One Thousand Secrets of Wise and Rich Men Revealed

# CONTENTS.

Chapter.
- I. Quick Shooting Records of C. A. Bogardus
- II. Medical Department
    - Accidents and Emergencies—What to Do
    - The Mind Cure
    - Poisons and Their Antidotes
- III. Ink Department
- IV. Cosmetic Department
- V. Live Stock Department
    - How to tell the Age of Horses, Cattle, etc.
- VI. Hog Department
- VII. Poultry Department
- VIII. Chemical Department
- IX. Miscellaneous Department
    - What to Invent, and How to Protect Your Invention
    - Candy—Directions for Making all Kinds of
- X. Coin Department—Illustrated List and Tables of Values of Rare Coins

Loisette's System of Memory

Useful Tables of Mnemonics

Facts Worth Knowing

Art Department

Gems of Thought from Poor Richard's Almanac, etc.

Robert Burns

# ANNOUNCEMENT.

SPRINGFIELD, MO., August 28th, 1907.

TO THE PUBLIC:

In as much as the former editions of this book have been so well liked, excepting the type being so small, it has been mentioned by many that a correction in that particular would be well. I have revised and enlarged the book and it now appears from larger type.

C. A. B.

# PREFACE.

Agesilaus, king of Sparta, being asked what things he thought most proper for *boys to learn*, replied: "Those things which they should *practice* when they become *men*." His reply was in perfect harmony with the good judgment of mankind, and cannot fail to be appreciated by all who have good common sense. If Agesilaus lived at the present time, the question would most probably have included both boys and girls, and undoubtedly his reply would be so worded as to apply to men and women.

Mankind, especially of the United States, has two great duties. First, that of self-support and education. Second, that of governmental support and national enlightenment. While I have thus divided man's responsibility in two parts, it might not be improper to obliviate the dividing line and say that man's duties are all under one comprehensive head, viz.: "Mankind's duty is to man." However, in the preparation of this volume the dividing line is recognized and two general departments are presented; that of domestic or household economy, and national or political economy. The former department is a compilation of useful household formulas so arranged and worded as to form a neat and concise household receipt book. Frequent reference to its pages will impart such information as will enable the reader to save money and at the same time enjoy life.

Department number two treats on social questions that are now knocking at humanity's intellectual threshold for admission and solution.

Records show that less than one-thirtieth part of the time of man in general is consumed in productive pursuits, yet some people toil diligently three-fifths of their time and receive only a scanty living. To assist in making clear the road to private and national prosperity is therefore the motive which actuates me in the publication of this book.

C. A. B.

# CHAPTER I.

## QUICK SHOOTING RECORDS.

From the time I was twelve years old I was considered a very fine shot with a rifle, although I did but very little shooting, and, in fact, did not know that I was any more than a common marksman; yet in any contests while a boy I always won.

One day in June, 1884, while passing a shooting gallery, my friends called me in for a match to pay for shots: I beat them all shooting, my score was 11 consecutive bull's eyes, while none of my friends had made half that score. The boys said I did well, to which I jestingly remarked that "that was common shooting for me; just throw up an apple and I will hit it." The apple was thrown up, and I hit it, which was as much of a surprise to me as it was to any of the rest. I then borrowed a 22-calibre Stevens rifle and practiced shooting at objects thrown in the air, first shooting at tomato cans, afterwards at smaller objects, and finally at marbles and various other small objects. By practicing half an hour a day, within a month I could hit 70 per cent of the glass balls which were thrown in the air. On July 4, 1884, I shot a match with James Robinson, at Pratt, Kansas; conditions, 10 glass balls each at 21 foot rise, he using a shot gun, I a rifle; I lost with a score of 4 to 6. This is the only match I ever lost with a rifle against a shot gun. The trouble with me was, this being my first match, I was thinking more about the stake money than the shooting. Besides the stake money which I lost, I had to treat all the boys who attended the match; they all laughed and had a good time at my expense.

The next day after my shoot with Robinson, I sent to P. Power & Son, of Cincinnati, for a 32-calibre Winchester repeating rifle. I continued practicing with the Winchester for about six weeks, when I challenged G. W. Washburn of Kingman, Kansas, to a match. (Mr. W. was at that time champion of Kingman County.) He to use a shot gun at glass balls from a Moles rotary trap, 21 yards rise, I to use a 32-calibre Winchester, balls from a straight trap, 10½ yards rise, 50 balls each. In the toss up I won and preferred to shoot second. The score was a tie on 47 balls; we shot the tie off at 10 balls each; again we tied on ten balls straight. The match was continued at 10 balls more each. By this time things had become a little exciting. Over $1500 was bet; many were betting $4 to $1 against me, thinking that I would lose my nerve and go to missing. Mr. W. walked to the score for the third time and broke 9 balls out of 10 shot at; it then came my turn to shoot, and I hit nine balls in succession when I was interrupted by a big fellow who offered to bet $25 I would miss the 10th ball; this bet was accepted, and it turned out that the fellow had just spoken in time to lose his $25, for the 10th ball had not got eight feet from the trap when I broke it. I won this match with a score of 67 against 66 out of 70 balls shot at. I then went to shooting at glass balls with rifle against a shot gun, and in the past 20 years I have competed against 206 good trap shots and have not lost a match. I will mention only a few of them. In the summer of '85, in Medicine Lodge, Kansas, an expert shooter came over from Cold Water, Kansas, to shoot with me. We had a match at target, distance 90 feet, with 22-calibre Stephens rifle; he used globe and peep sight, I used open sights. The score stood in my favor 114 to 107 out of a possible 120, at a quarter-inch bull's eye. The next day we shot a match at 100 glass balls, he using a shot gun, I a rifle. The score stood 99 to 94 in my favor. I will mention a match which I had in Omaha, Nebraska, in August, 1886. There was nothing very striking about this match because of fine shooting; I only mention it to show how unfair people sometimes are toward strangers. I have forgotten the man's name, but he was a barber working on Tenth street; he held a championship medal that he had won in Dakota with a Winchester rifle at glass balls. He challenged me to shoot three matches: First, 100 glass balls hanging still from the limb of a tree, fifty yards distance. Second match at 100 balls, 10 yards rise, thrown by hand. Third match, each to shoot 100 glass balls laid on the ground in a circle 200 feet in circumference, balls two feet apart, shooter to stand in the center of the circle, the one who broke the balls in the shortest time to win, but neither of us was allowed more than 133 shots in which to break the 100 balls. I had heard a good deal said of this man, over Nebraska everywhere he was spoken of as a fine shot, and in the first match I was really afraid of being beaten, for I never had practiced a great amount at stationary targets, but on the whole I was not afraid, for the party who won two out of the series of matches was to be declared the winner. In the first match I broke 100 balls in 206 shots, while my opponent broke 82 in the same number of shots; this made me easy winner of the first match. In the second match all kinds of tricks were resorted to, to beat me. My opponent's friends tried to rattle me by offering to bet that I would miss certain balls, but when they failed in this, the party throwing the balls would first throw a ball four feet high, then one 20 feet high, while my opponent's were thrown uniformly. Notwithstanding the fact that I was treated very unfair, the score stood a tie on 83 balls out of 100. In the third match at 100 balls in shortest time, I won easily, breaking the 100 balls in two minutes and three seconds, shooting 127 shots, while my opponent broke 61 balls in 133 shots, time four minutes, forty-two seconds. In Fort Smith, Arkansas, March 21, 1889, I shot on time at 100 glass balls against five men with shot guns, I using a 32-calibre Winchester rifle. I broke 100 balls in ninety-five seconds, while the five men broke 100 balls in three minutes and two seconds. Ravena, Ohio, July 4, 1890, I broke 250 glass balls in four minutes and sixteen seconds. At Newark, N.Y., July 4, 1891, I broke 81 glass balls in seventy-four seconds, 31 of which I broke in sixteen seconds, which is far the best record ever made with a rifle. In all of the matches I had assistants to load. I have hit 39 44-calibre cartridge shells out of 110 thrown up, 67 22-calibre cartridge shells out of 110 thrown up. The most difficult feat I ever performed was hitting 7 balls thrown up at one time. This I did at Shelby, Michigan, October 24, 1889, using a 44-calibre Winchester rifle loaded with shot cartridges. On July 4, 1893, I hit 1000 wooden balls with 22-calibre Marlin rifle in 17¼ minutes, which is 9.25 minutes quicker than the feat has ever been accomplished by any other person.

C. A. Bogardus

I have thrown an object into the air and hit it 12 times before it struck the ground, I using an automatic shot gun.

In concluding this article, I will suggest to those learning to shoot, that as a workman is known by the kind of tools he uses, it is equally true of the marksman. In order to do good shooting a good gun must be used. As a repeating rifle I have never seen the equal of the Marlin, model '92. When the gun is kept in good repair, used with well loaded cartridges, it is absolutely sure to repeat, a thing that I cannot say of any other repeating rifle. Although others are good, I consider the Marlin the *best*.

C. A. BOGARDUS,
*Champion Quick Shot of the World.*

# CHAPTER II.

## MEDICAL DEPARTMENT.[1]

BOGARDUS' LINIMENT.—Take two ozs. Oil Cajeput, one oz. Oil Sassafras, one oz. Oil Cloves, one oz. Oil Organum, ½-oz. Oil Mustard, one oz. Tinc. Capsicum, two ozs. Gum Camphor, one-half Gallon of Alcohol. Use as other liniments for any ache or pain. For sore throat or hoarseness, saturate a towel with the liniment, place it over the mouth, let it remain so for 4 or 5 hours, and you will be cured. For croup, bathe throat and chest with the liniment. Give one-fourth teaspoonful of liniment in one teaspoonful of warm water every 5 to 10 minutes till relieved. Also, let the child breathe the fumes of the liniment. I especially recommend this liniment for general family use.

HEALING SALVE.—One lb. Lard, ½ lb. Resin, ½ lb. Sweet Elder bark. Simmer over a slow fire 4 hours, or until it forms a hard, brown salve. This is for the cure of cuts, bruises, boils, old sores and all like ailments. Spread on a cotton cloth and apply to the parts affected.

SPECIFIC INFLAMMATORY RHEUMATISM.—One oz. Salt Petre, pulverized; one pint Sweet Oil. Bathe the parts affected three times a day with this mixture and a speedy cure will be the result.

ANOTHER SALVE.—One oz. Sheep's Tallow, Beeswax one oz., one-half oz. Sweet Oil, one-half oz. Red Lead, two ozs. Gum Camphor. Fry all these together in a stone dish. Continue to simmer for 4 hours. Spread on green basswood leaves or paper and apply to the sore.

MAGNETIC OINTMENT.—One lb. Elder Bark, one lb. Spikenard Root, one lb. Yellow Dock Root. Boil in two gallons of water down to one, then press the strength out of the bark and roots and boil the liquid down to one-half gallon. Add 8 lbs. of best Resin, one lb. Beeswax, and Tallow enough to soften. Apply to the sores, etc., by spreading on linen cloth.

OINTMENT STRAMONIUM.—One lb. Stramonium Leaves, three lbs. Lard, one-half lb. Yellow Wax. Boil the Stramonium Leaves in the Lard until they become pliable, then strain through linen. Lastly add the wax previously melted and stir until they are cold. This a useful anodyne application in irritable ulcers, painful hemorrhoids, and in cutaneous eruptions.

CATHARTIC PILLS.—One-half oz. extract Colacinth, in powder, three drms. Jolop in powder, three drms. Calomel, two scru. Gamboge in powder. Mix these together and with water form into mass and roll into 180 pills. Dose, one pill as a mild laxative, two in vigorous operations. Use in all bilious diseases when purges are necessary.

FOR HEARTBURN—LOZENGES.—One oz. Gum Arabic, one oz. pulverized Licorice Root, one-fourth oz. Magnesia. Add water to make into lozenges. Let dissolve in mouth and swallow.

ANOTHER COUGH CURE—(GOOD).—Take the white of an egg and pulverized sugar; beat to a froth. Take a tablespoonful every hour for 3 or 4 hours.

TETTER OINTMENT.—One oz. Spirits Turpentine, one ounce Red Precipitate in powder, one oz. Burgundy Pitch in powder, one lb. Hog's Lard. Melt all these ingredients over a slow fire until the ointment is formed. Stir until cold. Spread on a linen rag and apply to the parts affected.

A SURE CURE FOR PILES.—Confection of Senna, two ozs., Cream of Tartar one oz., Sulphur one oz., Syrup of Ginger, enough to make a stiff paste; mix. A piece as large as a nut is to be taken as often as necessary to keep the bowels open. One of the best remedies known.

DIPHTHERIA.—Take a clean clay tobacco pipe, put a live coal in it, then put common tar on the fire and smoke it, inhaling and breathing back through the nostrils.

FEVER AND AGUE.—Quinine one scru., Elixir Vitriol one drm. Dissolve the Quinine in the Elixir and Tinc. of Black Cohash fourteen drops. Dose: 20 drops in a little water once an hour.

CORNS.—A SURE CURE AND PAINLESS ERADICATION.—Extract of Cannabis Indicus ten grs., Salicylic Acid 6 grs., Collodion one oz. Mix and apply with a camel's hair pencil so as to form a thick covering over the corn for 3 or 4 nights. Take a hot foot bath and the corn can easily be removed with the aid of a knife.

MAGIC OIL.—One gallon Sweet Oil, two ozs. Oil Hemlock, two ozs. Oil Organum, two ozs. Chloroform, four ozs. Spirits Ammonia. Mix. Let it stand 24 hours and it is ready for use. Dose, internally, one teaspoonful for adults. Bathe the affected parts well. This is a great remedy for aches and pains, Rheumatism, Neuralgia, and all nervous and inflammatory diseases.

CURE FOR SORE THROAT IN ALL ITS DIFFERENT FORMS.—Two ozs. Cayenne Pepper, one oz. common Salt, one-half pint of Vinegar. Warm over a slow fire and gargle the throat and mouth every hour. Garlic and Onion poultice applied to the outside. Castor Oil, one spoonful to keep the bowels open.

DROPS OF LIFE.—One oz. Gum Opium, one drm. Gum Kino, forty grs. Gum Camphor, one-half ounce Nutmeg powdered, one pint French Brandy. Let stand from one to ten days. Dose, from 30 to 40 drops for an adult; children, half doses. This is one of the most valuable preparations in the Materia Medica, and will in some dangerous hours, when all hope is fled, and the system is racked with pain, be the soothing balm which cures the most dangerous disease to which the human body is liable—flux, dysentery and all summer complaints.

CATARRH, POSITIVE CURE.—Carbolic Acid, ten to twenty drops; Vaseline, one to two ozs. Mix and use with an atomizer 3 or 4 times per day.

COUGH DROPS.—Tinc. Aconite 5 drops, Tinc. Asclepias one drm., Glycerine two ozs., Syrup of Wild Cherry. Mix and take a teaspoonful every 40 minutes until relieved.

EYE WATER.—Table Salt and White Vitriol, each one teaspoonful. Heat them on earthen dish until dry. Now add them to soft water one-half pint. White Sugar one teaspoonful, Blue Vitriol a piece as large as a common pea. Should this be too strong add a little more water. Apply to the eye 3 or 4 times a day.

TO REMOVE TAPE WORM.—Let the patient miss two meals. Give two teaspoonfuls powdered Kamala. Should the bowels not move within two and-a half hours, give another teaspoonful of the Kamala. You may follow this in two hours by from half to one oz. Castor Oil. This is a positive cure for Tape Worm. It will not make the patient sick. In buying the drug be sure and get Kamala, not Camellea. Kamala is in appearance like quite red brick dust, and is nearly tasteless, whereas Camellea is of a yellowish color.

A SURE CURE FOR SMALL POX.—A gentleman contributes to the *ChicagoNews* the following as a sure and never failing cure for small pox: One ounce Cream of Tartar dissolved in pint of boiling water, to be drank when cold at intervals. It can be taken at any time, and as a preventive as well as a curative. It is known to have cured in thousands of cases without a failure.

TO STRENGTHEN AND INVIGORATE THE SYSTEM.—Two drms. Essential Salt of the Round Leaf Cornel, one scru. Extract Rhubarb, one scru. Ginger Powder. Make into pills, and take for a dose 2 or 3 twice a day.

GONORRHEA.—Balsam of Copabia one oz., Oil of Cubebs two drms., Laudanum one dram, Mucilage of Gum Arabic two ozs., Sweet Spirits Nitre half oz., Compound Spirits Lavender three drms., Camphor Water four ozs., White Sugar two drms., Oil of Partridge Berry five drops. Mix. Dose, a tablespoonful 3 or 4 times a day.

SURE CORN CURE.—One-half ounce Tincture of Iodine, one-half ounce Chloride or Antimony, 12 grains Iodide of Iron. Mix. Pare the corn with a sharp knife; apply the lotion with a pencil brush. Put up in one ounce bottles. Sell for 25 to 40 cents. This sells to everybody. (See price of labels.)

N.B.—The law imposing stamp duty on medicines, compounds, perfumes, cosmetics, etc., has been repealed.

RUSSIA SALVE.—Take equal parts of Yellow Wax and Sweet Oil, melt slowly, carefully stirring; when cooling stir in a small quantity of Glycerine. Good for all kinds of wounds, etc.

PARADISE LINIMENT.—Take a gill of Alcohol, one-fourth ounce Tincture Capsicum, one-half ounce Paradise Seed, cracked, and put all together. For rheumatism, sprains, lameness, etc.

COURT PLASTER.—This plaster is a kind of varnished silk, and its manufacture is very easy. Bruise a sufficient quantity of Isinglass, and let it soak in a little warm water for twenty-four hours. Expose it to heat over the fire until the greater part of the water is dissipated and supply its place by proof Spirits of Wine, which will combine with the Isinglass. Strain the whole through a piece of open linen, taking care that the consistency of the mixture shall be such that when cool it may form a trembling jelly. Extend a piece of black or flesh-colored silk on a wooden frame, and fix it in that position by means of tacks or twine. Then apply the Isinglass, after it has been rendered liquid by a gentle heat, to the silk with a brush of fine hair (badger's is the best). As soon as this coating is dried, which will not be long, apply a second, and afterward, if the article is to be very superior, a third. When the whole is dry, cover it with two or three coatings of the Balsam of Peru. This is the genuine court plaster. It is pliable and never breaks, which is far from being the case with spurious articles sold under the same name.

A CERTAIN CURE FOR DRUNKENNESS.—Sulphate of Iron five grains, Magnesia ten grains, Peppermint water eleven drachms, Spirits of Nutmeg, one drachm, twice a day. This preparation acts as a tonic and stimulant, and so partially supplies the place of the accustomed liquor, and prevents that absolute physical and mental prostration that follows a sudden breaking off from the use of stimulating drinks.

FRENCH LUSTRAL.—Take Castor Oil three ozs., Alcohol one and one-half ozs., Ammonia one-sixteenth of an oz., well shaken and mixed together; perfume to suit—Bergamont or any other perfume. Splendid hair dressing. Three ounce bottles, twenty-five cents.

LUNG MEDICINE.—Take Black Cohosh one-half oz., Lobelia one-fourth oz., Canker root three-fourths oz., Blackberry Root three-fourths of an oz., Sarsaparilla one oz., Pleurisy Root one-half oz., steeped in three pints of water. Dose, one tablespoonful three times a day, before eating. Sure cure for spitting blood.

TOOTHACHE DROPS.—Four ounces pulverized Alum, fourteen ozs. Sweet Spirits of Nitre. Put up in one oz. bottles. Retails readily at 25 cents per bottle. This is the most effective remedy for toothache that was ever discovered, and is a fortune to any one who will push its sale. It sells at every house.

MAGNETIC TOOTHACHE DROPS.—Take equal parts of Camphor, Sulphuric Ether, Ammonia, Laudanum, Tincture of Cayenne, and one-eighth part of Oil of Cloves. Mix well together. Saturate with the liquid a small piece of cotton, and apply to the cavity of the diseased tooth, and the pain will cease immediately. Put up in long drachm bottles. Retail at 25 cents. This is a very salable preparation, and affords a large profit to the manufacturer.

GREEN MOUNTAIN SALVE.—Take one pound Beeswax, one pound of soft Butter, and one and one-half pounds soft Turpentine, twelve ounces Balsam Fir. Melt and strain. Use to heal fresh wounds, burns, scalds and all bad sores.

WARTS AND CORNS—TO CURE IN TEN MINUTES.—Take a small piece of Potash and let it stand in the open air until it slacks, then thicken it to a paste with pulverized Gum Arabic, which prevents it from spreading where it is not wanted.

LINIMENT—GOOD SAMARITAN.—Take 98 per cent Alcohol two quarts, and add to it the following articles: Oils of Sassafras, Hemlock, Spirits of Turpentine, Tincture Cayenne, Catechu, Guaic (guac), and Laudanum, of each one ounce, Tincture of Myrrh four ounces, Oil of Organum two ounces, Oil of Wintergreen one-half ounce. Gum Camphor two ounces, and Chloroform one and one-half ounce. This is one of the best applications for internal pains known. It is superior to any other enumerated in this work.

PLAIN COURT PLASTER, that will not stick and remains flexible: Soak Isinglass in a little warm water for twenty-four hours, then evaporate nearly all the water by gentle heat. Dissolve the residue with a little Proof Spirits of Wine, and strain the whole through a piece of open linen. The strained mass should be a stiff jelly when cool. Stitch a piece of silk or sarcenet on a wooden frame with tacks or thread. Melt the jelly and apply it to the silk thinly and evenly with a badger hair brush. A second coating must be applied after the first has dried. When the both are dry apply over the whole surface two or three coatings of Balsam of Peru. This plaster remains quite pliable, and never breaks.

A CURE FOR CANCER (AS USED BY A NEW YORK PHYSICIAN WITH GREAT SUCCESS).—Take Red Oak Bark, and boil it to the thickness of molasses, then mix with sheep's tallow of equal proportion. Spread it on leaves of Linnwood green, and keep the plaster over the ulcer. Change once in eight hours.

DAVIS' PAIN KILLER—One quart proof Alcohol, one drm., Chloroform, one oz. Oil Sassafras, one oz. Gum Camphor, one drm. Spirits of Ammonia, two drms. Oil of Cayenne. Mix well and let stand 24 hours before using.

AUGUST FLOWER.—Powdered Rhubarb one oz., Golden Seal one-fourth oz., Aloes one drachm, Peppermint Leaves two drms., Carbonate of Potash two drms., Capsicum five grs., Sugar five ozs., Alcohol three ozs., Water ten ozs., Essence of Peppermint twenty drops. Powder the drugs and let stand covered with Alcohol and water, equal parts for seven days. Filter and add through the filter enough diluted Alcohol to make one pint.

BLOOD PURIFIER—B.B.B.—Fluid Extract Burdock one oz., Fluid Extract Sarsaparilla one oz., Fluid Extract Yellow Dock one oz., Fluid Extract Senna one oz., Syrup eight ozs., Alcohol two ozs. Mix.

BOSCHEE'S GERMAN SYRUP.—Wine of Tar two ozs., Fluid Extract Squills one oz., Tinct. Opium two drms., Fluid Extract Sanguinarie two drms., Syrup of Sugar eight ozs. Mix.

CENTAUR LINIMENT.—Oil Speke one oz., Oil Wormwood one oz., Oil Sassafras one oz., Oil Organum one oz., Oil Cinnamon one oz., Oil Cloves one drm., Oil Cedar one drm., Sulphur. Ether one oz., Aqua Ammonia one oz., Tinc. Opium one oz., Alcohol one gal. Mix. This is an excellent liniment and good whenever a liniment is needed.

CASTORIA.—Pumpkin Seed one oz., Cenria Leaves one oz., Rochelle Salts one oz., Anise Seed one-half oz., Bi. Carb. Soda one oz., Worm Seed one-half oz. Mix and thoroughly rub together in an earthen vessel, then put into a bottle and pour over it four ozs. water and one oz. Alcohol, and let stand four days, then strain off and add Syrup made of White Sugar, quantity to make one pint, then add one-half oz. Alcohol drops and five drops Wintergreen. Mix thoroughly and add to the contents of the bottle and take as directed.

HARTER'S IRON TONIC.—Calisaya Bark two ozs., Citrate of Iron two ozs., Gentian two ozs., Cardamon Seed two ozs., Syrup two ozs., Alcohol two ozs., Water eight ozs. Mix.

HALL'S BALSAM FOR THE LUNGS.—Fluid Extract Ipecac one-half oz., Fluid Extract Squills one oz., Chloroform one-fourth oz., Wine of Tar one oz., Tinct. Opium, one-fifth oz., Fluid Extract of Mullen one oz., Syrup enough to make one pint.

GODFREY'S CORDIAL.—Tinct. Opium six ozs., Molasses four pints, Alcohol eight ozs., Water six pints, Carbonate Potash four drms., Oil Sassafras cut with Alcohol one drm. Dissolve the Potash in water, add the Molasses; heat over a gentle fire till it simmers, remove the scum, add the other ingredients, the oil dissolved in the Alcohol.

HALL'S HONEY OF HOARHOUND AND TAR.—Wine of Tar one oz., Fluid Extract of Hoarhound one oz., Tinct. Opium one drm., Syrup Orange Peel one-half oz., Honey three ozs., Syrup enough to make one pint.

HOOD'S SARSAPARILLA.—Fluid Extract Sarsaparilla one oz., Fluid Extract Yellow Dock one oz., Fluid Extract Poke Root, one-half oz., Iodide of Potash one-half oz., Syrup Orange Peel one oz., Alcohol four ozs., Syrup enough to make one pint.

HAMLIN'S WIZARD OIL.—Oil Sassafras two ozs., Oil Cedar one oz., Gum Camphor one oz., Sulph. Ether two ozs., Chloroform two ozs., Tinct. Capsicum one oz., Aqua Ammonia two ozs., Oil Turpentine one oz., Tinct. Quassia three ozs., Alcohol half a gallon. Mix and you have a fine liniment.

HOP BITTERS.—Hops four ozs., Orange Peel two ozs., Cardamon two drms., Cinnamon one drm., Cloves one-half drm., Alcohol eight ozs., Sherry Wine two pints, Simple Syrup one pint. Water sufficient. Grind the drugs, macerate in the Alcohol and Wine for one week, percolate and add enough syrup and water to make one gallon.

HOSTETTER'S BITTERS.—Gentian Root (ground) one-half oz., Cinnamon Bark one-half oz., Cinchona Bark (ground) one-half oz., Anise Seed one-half oz., Coriander Seed (ground) one-half oz., Cardamon Seed one-eighth oz., Gum Kino one-fourth oz., Alcohol one pint. Water four quarts, Sugar one lb. Mix and let stand for one week, pour off the fluid, boil the drug for a few minutes in one quart of water, strain off and add the first fluid, and then the sugar and water.

INJECTION BROU.—Water four ozs., Nitrate Silver twenty grs., Tinct. Opium one-half oz., Sulph. Bismuth and Hydratis two oz. Mix.

JAYNE'S EXPECTORANT.—Syrup Squills two ozs., Tinct. Tolu one oz., Spirits Camphor one drm., Tinct. Digitalis one drm., Tinct. Lobelia one drm., Wine of Ipecac two drms., Tinc. Opium two drms., Antimonia two grains. Mix.

JAYNE'S TONIC VERMIFUGE.—L. santonnie twenty grs., Fluid Extract Pink Root three drms., Fluid Extract Senna two drms., Simple Elixir two ozs., Syrup two ozs. Mix. Take tablespoonful night and morning.

MUSTANG LINIMENT.—Linseed Oil fourteen ozs., Aqua Ammonia two ozs., Tinct. Capsicum one-fourth oz., Oil Organum one-fourth oz., Turpentine one oz., Oil Mustard, one-fourth oz. Mix.

S.S.S. FLUID.—Extract Phytolacca one oz., Fluid Extract Sarsaparilla one oz., Iodide Potash one oz., Extract Fluid Xanthoxylon one-half oz., Culiver's Root Fluid Extract one oz., Acetate Potash one oz., Cinnamon Tinct. one-fourth oz., Tinct. Cardamon Seed one oz., Alcohol four ozs., Sugar one-half pound, Water thirty-six ozs. Mix.

SMITH'S TONIC.—Fowler's Solution of Arsenic two drms., Culiver's Root one oz., Syrup Orange Peel four ozs., Simple Syrup twelve ozs. Mix. Then add Chinchonia forty grains dissolved in Aromatic Sulph. Acid. Shake to mix well.

SOZODONT FRAGRANT.—Tinct. Soap Bark two ozs., Tinct. Myrrh one drm., Glycerine one-half oz., Water one and one-half ozs., Essence Cloves ten drops, Essence Wintergreen ten drops, Tinct. Cochineal enough to color. Mix. Accompanying the above is a powder composed of prepared Chalk, Orris Root, Carbonate Magnesia, of each equal parts. Mix.

SHAKER'S CUTIVE SYRUP.—Fluid Extract Blue Flag twenty drops, Fluid Extract Culiver's Root twenty drops, Fluid Extract Poke Root twenty drops, Fluid Extract Butternut twenty drops, Fluid Extract Dandelion twenty drops, Fluid Extract Prince Pine ten drops, Fluid Extract Mandrake five drops, Fluid Extract Gentian five drops, Fluid Extract Calcium five drops, Fluid Extract Black Cohoes thirty drops, Tinct. Aloe thirty drops, Tinct. Capsicum ten drops, Tinct. Sassafras thirty drops, Borax one drm., Salt three-fourths drm., Syrup three ozs., Water eight ozs.

AYER'S CHERRY PECTORAL.—Take four grains of Acetate of Morphia, two fluid drachms of Tincture of Bloodroot, three fluid drachms each of Antimonial Wine and Wine of Ipecacuanha, and three fluid ounces Syrup of Wild Cherry. Mix.

BROWN'S BRONCHIAL TROCHES.—Take one pound pulverized Extract of Licorice, one and one-half pounds Pulverized Sugar, four ounces pulverized Cubebs, four ounces pulverized Gum Arabic, and one ounce of pulverized Extract of Conium. Mix.

SUCCUS ALTERNS (McDADE'S).—Fluid Extract Starlinga one oz., Fluid Extract Sarsaparilla one oz., Fluid Extract Phytolacca Decandra one-half oz., Fluid Extract Lappa Minor one oz., Fluid Extract Xanthoxylon one-half oz., Syrup fourteen ozs., Mix. Teaspoonful three times a day.

SEVEN SEALS OF GOLDEN WONDER.—Oil Cajeput two drms., Sassafras one-half oz., Oil Organum one drm., Oil Hemlock one drm., Oil Cedar one drm., Tincture Capsicum one-fourth oz., Alcohol enough to make one pint.

WAKEFIELD'S WINE BITTERS.—Cinchona Bark four ozs., Gentian Bark two ozs., Juniper Berries one oz., Orange Peel one oz., Lemon Peel fresh sliced one-fourth oz., California Port Wine four pints, Alcohol one pint, Water three pints. Digest or let stand ten days, then filter and add wine enough to preserve measure.

ST. JACOB'S OIL.—Camphor Gum one oz., Chloral Hydrate one oz., Chloroform one oz., Sulphate Ether one oz., Tinct. Opium (non-aqueous) one-half oz., Oil Organum one-half oz., Oil Sassafras one-half oz., Alcohol one-half gallon. Dissolve Gum Camphor with Alcohol and then add the oil, then the other ingredients.

R.R.R.—Alcohol two pints, Oil Sassafras two ozs., Oil Organum twi ozs., Camphor Spirits one-half oz., Tinct. Opium one oz., Chloroform one oz. Mix.

PISO'S CONSUMPTION CURE.—Tartar Emetic four grains, Tinc. Tolu one-half oz., Sulphate Morphia four grains, Fluid Extract Lobelia two drms., Chloroform one drm., Fluid Extract Cannabis Indica two drms., Essence Spearmint ten drops, Hot Water eight ozs., Sugar four ozs., Dissolve the Morphia and Tartar Emetic in hot water and add the rest.

WARNER'S TIPPECANOE BITTERS.—Cardamon Seed two ozs., Nutmeg one drm., Grains of Paradise one drm., Cloves one oz., Cinnamon two ozs., Ginger one oz., Orange Peel one oz., Lemon Peel one oz., Alcohol one gallon, Water one gallon, Sugar three pounds. Mix and let stand for six or seven days and filter. Then add enough water to make four gallons.

WARNER'S SAFE CURE.—Take of Smart Weed four pounds, boil for one hour with one gallon soft water, adding warm water to supply waste by evaporation; then strain off and add Acetate Potash four ozs., Sugar four pounds. Boil again till sugar is dissolved, then add Alcohol eight ozs., and flavor with Oil of Wintergreen cut with Alcohol.

WAKEFIELD'S BLACKBERRY BALSAM.—Blackberries crushed two pounds, Boiling Water four ozs., Sugar four ozs., Jamaica Ginger four grs., Alcohol two ozs. Mix and add Syrup enough to make sixteen ozs.

## ACCIDENTS AND EMERGENCIES.

### WHAT TO DO.

If an artery is cut, red blood spurts. Compress it above the wound. If a vein is cut, dark blood flows. Compress it below and above.

If choked, go upon all fours and cough.

For slight burns, dip the part in cold water; if the skin is destroyed, cover with varnish or linseed oil.

For apoplexy, raise the head and body; for fainting, lay the person flat.

Send for a physician when a serious accident of any kind occurs, but treat as directed until he arrives.

SCALDS AND BURNS.—The following facts cannot be too firmly impressed on the mind of the reader, that in either of these accidents the *first, best* and *often the only remedies required*, are sheets of wadding, fine wool, or carded cotton, and in the default of these, violet powder, flour, magnesia or chalk. The object for which these several articles are employed is the same in each instance; namely, to exclude the air from injured part; for if the air can be effectually shut out from the raw surface, and care is taken not to expose the tender part till the new cuticle is formed, the cure may be safely left to nature. The moment a person is called to a case of scald or burn, he should cover the part with a sheet, or a portion of a sheet, of wadding, taking care not to break any blister that may have formed, or stay to remove any burnt clothes that may adhere to the surface, but as quickly as possible envelope every part of the injury from all access of the air, laying one or two more pieces of wadding on the first, so as to effectually guard the burn or scald from the irritation of the atmosphere; and if the article used is wool or cotton, the same precaution, of adding more material where the surface is thinly covered, must be adopted; a light bandage finally securing all in their places. Any of the popular remedies recommended below may be employed when neither wool, cotton nor wadding are to be procured, it being always remembered that that article which will best exclude the air from a burn or scald is the best, quickest, and least painful mode of treatment. And in this respect nothing has surpassed cotton loose or attached to paper as in wadding.

*If the Skin is Much Injured* in burns, spread some linen pretty thickly with chalk ointment, and lay over the part, and give the patient some brandy and water if much exhausted; then send for a medical man. If not much injured, and very painful, use the same ointment, or apply carded cotton dipped in lime water and linseed oil. If you please, you may lay cloths dipped in ether over the parts, or cold lotions. Treat scalds in same manner, or cover with scraped raw potato; but the chalk ointment is the best. In the absence of all these, cover the injured part with treacle, and dust over it plenty of flour.

BODY IN FLAMES.—Lay the person down on the floor of the room, and throw the table cloth, rug or other large cover over him, and roll him on the floor.

DIRT IN THE EYE.—Place your forefinger upon the cheek-bone, having the patient before you; then slightly bend the finger, this will draw down the lower lid of the eye, and you will probably be able to remove the dirt; but if this will not enable you to get at it, repeat this operation while you have a netting needle or bodkin placed over the eyelid; this will turn it inside out, and enable you to remove the sand or eyelash, etc., with the corner of a fine silk handkerchief. As soon as the substance is removed, bathe the eye with cold water, and exclude the light for a day. If the inflammation is severe, let the patient use a refrigerant lotion.

LIME IN THE EYE.—Syringe it well with warm vinegar and water in the proportion of one ounce of vinegar to eight ounces of water; exclude light.

IRON OR STEEL SPICULAE IN THE EYE.—These occur while turning iron or steel in a lathe, and are best remedied by doubling back the upper or lower eyelid, according to the situation of the substance, and with the flat edge of a silver probe, taking up the metallic particle, using a lotion made by dissolving six grains of sugar of lead and the same of white vitriol, in six ounces of water, and bathing the eye three times a day till the inflammation subsides. Another plan is—Drop a solution of sulphate of copper (from one to three grains of the salt to one ounce of water) into the eye, or keep the eye open in a wineglassful of the solution. Bathe with cold lotion, and exclude light to keep down inflammation.

DISLOCATED THUMB.—This is frequently produced by a fall. Make a clove hitch, by passing two loops of cord over the thumb, placing a piece or rag under the cord to prevent it cutting the thumb; then pull in the same line as the thumb. Afterwards apply a cold lotion.

CUTS AND WOUNDS.—Clean cut wounds, whether deep or superficial, and likely to heal by the first intention, should always be washed or cleaned, and at once evenly and smoothly closed by bringing both edges close together, and securing them in that position by adhesive plaster. Cut thin strips of sticking plaster, and bring the parts together; or if large and deep, cut two broad pieces, so as to look like the teeth of a comb, and place one on each side of the wound, which must be cleaned previously. These pieces must be arranged so that they will interlace one another; then, by laying hold of the pieces on the right side with one hand, and those on the other side with the other hand, and pulling them from one another, the edges of the wound are brought together without any difficulty.

*Ordinary Cuts* are dressed by thin strips, applied by pressing down the plaster on one side of the wound, and keeping it there and pulling in the opposite direction; then suddenly depressing the hand when the edges of the wound are brought together.

CONTUSIONS are best healed by laying a piece of folded lint, well wetted with extract of lead, or boracic acid, on the part, and, if there is much pain, placing a hot bran poultice over the dressing, repeating both, if necessary, every two hours. When the injuries are very severe, lay a cloth over the part, and suspend a basin over it filled with cold lotion. Put a piece of cotton into the basin, so that it shall allow the lotion to drop on the cloth, and thus keep it always wet.

HEMORRHAGE, when caused by an artery being divided or torn, may be known by the blood issuing out of the wound in leaps or jerks, and being of a bright scarlet color. If a vein is injured, the blood is darker and flows continuously. To arrest the latter, apply pressure by means of a compress and bandage. To arrest arterial bleeding, get a piece of wood (part of a broom handle will do), and tie a piece of tape to one end of it; then tie a piece of tape loosely over the arm, and pass the other end of the wood under it; twist the stick round and round until the tape compresses the arm sufficiently to arrest the bleeding, and then confine the other end by tying the string around the arm. A compress made by enfolding a penny piece in several folds of lint or linen should, however, be first placed under the tape and over the artery. If the bleeding is very obstinate, and it occurs in the *arm*, place a cork underneath the string, on the inside of the fleshy part, where the artery may be felt beating by anyone, if in the *leg*, place a cork in the direction of a line drawn from the inner part of the knee towards the outer part of the groin. It is an excellent thing to accustom yourself to find out the position of these arteries, or, indeed, any that are superficial, and to explain to every person in your house where they are, and how to stop bleeding. If a stick cannot be got, take a handkerchief, make a cord bandage of it, and tie a knot in the middle; the knot acts as a compress, and should be placed over the artery, while the two ends are to be tied around the thumb. Observe *always to place the ligature between the wound and the heart*. Putting your finger into a bleeding wound, and making pressure until a surgeon arrives, will generally stop violent bleeding.

BLEEDING FROM THE NOSE, from whatever cause, may generally be stopped by putting a plug of lint into the nostrils; if this does not do, apply a cold lotion to the forehead; raise the head, and place over it both arms, so that it will rest on the hands; dip the lint plug, *slightlymoistened*, into some powdered Gum Arabic, and plug the nostrils again; or dip the plug into equal parts of powdered Gum Arabic and alum, and plug the nose. Or the plug may be dipped in Friar's balsam, or tincture of Kino. Heat should be applied to the feet; and, in obstinate cases, the sudden shock of a cold key, or cold water poured down the spine, will instantly stop the bleeding. If the bowels are confined take a purgative. Injections of alum solution from a small syringe into the nose will often stop hemorrhage.

VIOLENT SHOCKS will sometimes stun a person, and he will remain unconscious. Untie strings, collars, etc.; loosen anything that is tight, and interferes with the breathing; raise the head; see if there is bleeding from any part; apply smelling salts to the nose, and hot bottles to the feet.

IN CONCUSSION, the surface of the body is cold and pale, and the pulse weak and small, the breathing slow and *gentle*, and the pupil of the eye generally contracted or small. You can get an answer by speaking loud, so as to rouse the patient. Give a little brandy and water, keep the place quiet, apply warmth, and do not raise the head too high. If you tickle the feet, the patient feels it.

IN COMPRESSION OF THE BRAIN from any cause, such as apoplexy, or a piece of fractured bone pressing on it, there is loss of sensation. If you tickle the feet of the injured person he does not feel it. You cannot arouse him so as to get an answer. The pulse is slow and labored; the breathing deep, labored, and *snorting*; the pupil enlarged. Raise the head, loosen strings or tight things, and send for a surgeon. If one cannot be got at once, apply mustard poultices to the feet and thighs, leeches to the temples, and hot water to the feet.

CHOKING.—When a person has a fish bone in the throat, insert the forefinger, press upon the root of the tongue, so as to induce vomiting; if this does not do, let him swallow a large piece of potato or soft bread; and if these fail, give a mustard emetic.

FAINTING, HYSTERICS, ETC.—Loosen the garments, bathe the temples with water or eau-de-Cologne; open the window, admit plenty of fresh air, dash cold water on the face, apply hot bricks to the feet, and avoid bustle and excessive sympathy.

DROWNING.—Attend to the following *essentialrules* : 1. Lose no time. 2. Handle the body gently. 3. Carry the body face downwards, with the head gently raised, and never hold it up by the feet. 4. Send for medical assistance immediately, and in the meantime act as follows: 5. Strip the body; rub it dry, then wrap it in hot blankets, and place it in a warm bed in a warm room. 6. Cleanse away the froth and mucous from the nose and mouth. 7. Apply warm bricks, bottles, bags of sand, etc., to the arm pits, between the thighs, and to the soles of the feet. 8. Rub the surface of the body with the hands inclosed in warm, dry worsted socks. 9. If possible, put the body into a warm bath. 10. To restore breathing, put the pipe of a common bellows into one nostril, carefully closing the other, and the mouth; at the same time drawing downwards, and pushing gently backwards, the upper part of the windpipe, to allow a more free admission of air; blow the bellows gently, in order to inflate the lungs, till the breast is raised a little; then set the mouth and nostrils free, and press gently on the chest; repeat this until signs of life appear. The body should be covered from the moment it is placed on the table, except the face, and all the rubbing carried on under the sheet or blanket. When they can be obtained, a number of tiles or bricks should be made tolerably hot in the fire, laid in a row on the table, covered with a blanket, and the body placed in such a manner on them that their heat may enter the spine. When the patient revives, apply smelling-salts to the nose, give warm wine or brandy and water. *Cautions.*—1. Never rub the body with salt or spirits. 2. Never roll the body on casks. 3. Continue the remedies for twelve hours without ceasing.

HANGING.—Loosen the cord, or whatever it may be by which the person has been suspended. Open the temporal artery or jugular vein, or bleed from the arm; employ electricity, if at hand, and proceed as for drowning, taking the additional precaution to apply eight or ten leeches to the temples.

APPARENT DEATH FROM DRUNKENNESS—Raise the head, loosen the clothes, maintain warmth of surface, and give a mustard emetic as soon as the person can swallow.

APOPLEXY AND FITS GENERALLY.—Raise the head; loosen all tight clothes, strings, etc.; apply cold lotions to the head, which should be shaved; apply leeches to the temples, bleed, and send for a surgeon.

SUFFOCATION FROM NOXIOUS GASES, ETC.—Remove to the fresh air; dash cold vinegar and water in the face, neck, and breast; keep up the warmth of the body; if necessary, apply mustard poultices to the soles of the feet and to the spine, and try artificial respirations as in drowning, with electricity.

LIGHTNING AND SUNSTROKE.—Treat the same as apoplexy.

## MIND CURE.

THE MIND CURE, otherwise known in its various subdivisions as metaphysics, Christian science, mental science, etc., is a species of delusion quite popular at the present time. Every era of the world has cherished similar delusions, for the mass of the human race, even in what are considered the educated classes, are so unfamiliar with the processes of exact reasoning that they fall a ready prey to quacks of all kinds. The fundamental idea of the mind cure system is that there is no such thing as sickness. Disease, says one of their apostles, is an error of the mind, the result of fear. Fear is only faith inverted and perverted. God, who is all good Himself, and who made everything good, cannot have been the author of any disease. As disease, therefore, is not a creation, it has no existence, and when the healer has succeeded in impressing this fact upon the mind of the patient, the cure is effected. It is curious to note into what utter absurdities the need for consistency carries these apostles. Poisons, they say, would be quite harmless if the fear of them was removed, but we have yet to find the "mental science" teacher who will undertake to prove this by herself taking liberal doses of aconite and strychnine. The illnesses of children are explained by the hypothesis of hereditary fear. The majority of the teachers of this new faith are women, many of whom, no doubt, are sincere in their belief; but it may be safely stated that the men engaged as the so-called physicians of the new practice are, with few exceptions, unprincipled quacks, who have gone into the business for the money they can make by duping the ignorant. As far as there is any truth underlying the vagaries of mind cures, and their boasts of remarkable cases of healing, it may be admitted that the mind has much influence over the body. This fact has been recognized by intelligent physicians for centuries. And that the peculiar modern type of nervous diseases, which are so largely caused by excessive stimulus of the nerves and the imagination, should be amendable to cure through the imagination, is not strange. It will be noted that this mental cure has effected its miracles mainly among women, where it has the emotional temperament to work on, and almost wholly in the ranks of the wealthy and well-to-do, where there is little or no impoverishment of the system by insufficient food and excessive toil to hinder its effects. We have not heard, nor are we likely to hear, of an epidemic disease checked by the mind cure, or of the healing of acute affections or organic troubles through its agency. Nor do we hear of its seeking to carry its message of healing into the houses of the suffering poor in large cities, where hunger, exposure and foul airs open wide the door to fevers and all deadly diseases, nor yet into the hospitals for contagious or incurable affections. In the presence of such realities it would prove, as its votaries probably understand, a too-painful mockery. Intelligently analyzed, therefore, this new revelation amounts to nothing more than a quite striking proof of the remarkable influence of the mind over the nervous system. Beyond this, the craze, in attempting to disprove the existence of disease, and to show that poisons do not kill, is simply running against the plain and inevitable facts of life, and can safely be left to perish through its own rashness.

While it must be admitted that many upright and worthy people are followers of this faith, it can be asserted that to say "disease is only a mental derangement" is carrying the idea of the power of mind over matter entirely too far.

## POISONS AND THEIR ANTIDOTES.

Always send immediately for a medical man. Save all fluids vomited, and articles of food, cups, glasses, etc., used by the patient before taken ill, and lock them up.

As a rule give emetics after poisons that cause sleepiness and raving; chalk, milk, eggs, butter and warm water, or oil, after poisons that cause vomiting and pain in the stomach and bowels, with purging; and when there is no inflammation about the throat, tickle it with a feather to excite vomiting.

Vomiting may be caused by giving warm water, with a teaspoonful of mustard to the tumblerful, well stirred up. Sulphate of zinc (white vitriol) may be used in place of the mustard, or powdered alum. Powder of ipecacuanha, a teaspoonful rubbed up with molasses, may be employed for children. *Tartar emetic should never be given*, as it is excessively depressing, and uncontrolable in its effects. The stomach pump can only be used by skillful hands, and even then with caution.

*Opium and Other Narcotics.*—After vomiting has occurred, cold water should be *dashed* over the face and head. The patient must be kept awake, walked about between two strong persons, made to grasp the handles of a galvanic battery, dosed with strong coffee, and vigorously slapped. *Belladonna* is an antidote for opium and for morphia, etc., its active principles; and, on the other hand, the latter counteract the effects of belladonna. But a knowledge of medicine is necessary for dealing with these articles.

*Strychnia.*—After emetics have been freely and successfully given, the patient should be allowed to breathe the vapor of sulphuric ether, poured on a handkerchief and held to the face, in such quantities as to keep down the tendency to convulsions. Bromide of potassium, twenty grains at a dose, dissolved in syrup, may be given every hour.

*Alcoholic Poisoning* should be combated by emetics, of which the sulphate of zinc given as above directed, is the best. After that, strong coffee internally, and stimulation by heat externally, should be used.

*Acids* are sometimes swallowed by mistake. Alkalies, lime water, magnesia, or common chalk mixed with water, may be freely given, and afterward mucilaginous drinks, such as thick gum water or flaxseed tea.

*Alkalies* are less frequently taken in injurious strength or quantity, but sometimes children swallow lye by mistake. Common vinegar may be given freely, and then castor or sweet oil in full doses—a tablespoonful at a time, repeated every half hour or two.

*NitrateofSilver* when swallowed is neutralized by common table salt freely given in solution in water.

The salts of *mercury* or *arsenic* (often kept as bedbug poison), which are powerful irritants, are apt to be very quickly fatal. Milk or the whites of eggs may be freely given, and afterward a very thin paste of flour is neutralized.

*Phosphorus* paste, kept for roach poison or in parlor matches, is sometimes eaten by children, and has been wilfully taken for the purpose of suicide. It is a powerful irritant. The first thing to be done is to give freely of magnesia and water; then to give mucilaginous drinks, as flaxseed tea, gum water or sassafras pith and water; and lastly to administer finely-powdered bone-charcoal, either in pill or in mixture with water.

In no case of poisoning should there be any avoidable delay in obtaining the advice of a physician, and, meanwhile, the friends or by-standers should endeavor to find out exactly what has been taken, so that the treatment adopted may be as prompt and effective as possible.

# CHAPTER III.

## INK DEPARTMENT.

RED INK.—Two ounces Cochineal, bruised; pour over it one quart Boiling Water, let it stand eight hours. Boil two ounces Brazil Wood in one pint of Water, let it stand eight hours and then add the two together. Dissolve one-half ounce Gum Arabic in one-half pint Hot Water; add all together and let stand four days. Strain and bottle for use.

BLUE INK.—Six parts Persian Blue, one quart Oxalic Acid; triturate with little Water to smoothe paste, add Gum Arabic and the necessary quantity of Water.

INDELIBLE INK TO MARK LINEN.—One and a half ounces Nitrate of Silver dissolved in six ounces Liquor Ammonia Fortis, one ounce Archill, for coloring; one-half ounce Gum Arabic. Mix.

FOR YELLOW.—Write with Muriate of Antimony; when dry wash with Tincture of Galls.

BLACK.—Write with a Solution of Green Vitriol and wash with Tincture of Galls.

BLUE.—Nitrate of Cobate, wash with Oxalic Acid.

YELLOW.—Subacetate of Lead, wash with Hydrochloric Acid.

GREEN.—Arsenate of Potash, wash with Nitrate of Copper.

PURPLE.—Solution of Gold and Muriate of Tin.

BLACK.—Perchloride of Mercury, the wash is Hydrochloric of Tin.

BLACK INK.—Extract of Logwood one ounce, Bicromate of Potash one-quarter ounce. Pulverize and mix in a quart of soft hot water. This makes a beautiful jet black ink, which will not spoil by freezing.

COPYING INK.—One-half gallon of soft water, one ounce Gum Arabic, one ounce Brown Sugar, one ounce clean Copperas, three ounces powdered Nut Gall. Mix and shake occasionally from 7 to 10 days and strain. The best copying ink made.

BLACK INK.—Shellac four ounces, Borax two ounces, Water one quart; boil till dissolved and add two ounces Gum Arabic, dissolved in a little hot water; boil and add enough of a well triturated mixture of equal parts of Indigo and Lampblack to produce a copper color. After standing several hours draw off and bottle.

GREEN INK.—Dissolve 180 grains Bichromate of Potash in one fluid ounce of Water; add while warm one-half ounce Spirits of Wine, then decompose the mixture with concentrated sulphuric acid until it assumes a brown color; evaporate this liquid until its quantity is reduced one-half, dilute it with two ounces distilled water, filter it, add one-half ounce Alcohol, followed by a few drops of strong sulphuric acid; it is now allowed to rest, and after a time it assumes a beautiful green color. Add a small quantity Gum Arabic and it is ready for use.

BEAUTIFUL BLUE WRITING FLUID.—Dissolve Basic or Soluble Prussian Blue in pure water. This is the most permanent and beautiful blue ink known.

VIOLET COPYING INK.—For blue violet dissolve in 300 parts of boiling water, Methyl Violet, 5 B, Hofman's Violet, 3 B, or Gentiana Violet, B. For reddish violet dissolve in a similar quantity of water Methyl Violet BR. A small quantity of sugar added to these inks improves their copying qualities.

If the writing when dry retains a bronzy appearance, more water must be added.

NEW INVISIBLE INK.—C. Wideman communicates a new method of making an invisible ink to *Die Natur*. To make the writing or drawing appear which has been made upon paper it is sufficient to dip it in water. On drying the traces disappear again, and reappear again at each succeeding immersion. The ink is made by intimately mixing Linseed Oil one part. Water of Ammonia twenty parts, Water 100 parts. The mixture must be agitated each time before the pen is dipped into it, as a little of the oil may separate and float on top, which would, of course, leave an oily stain upon the paper.

BUCHER'S CARMINE INK.—Pure Carmine, twelve grains, Water of Ammonia three ounces, dissolve, then add Powdered Gum eighteen grains. One-half drachm of Powdered Drop Lake may be substituted for the Carmine, where expense is an object.

BRILLIANT RED INK.—Brazil Wood two ounces, Muriate of Tin one-half drachm, Gum Arabic one drachm. Boil down in 32 ounces water to one-half, and strain.

WHITE INK.—Mix pure freshly precipitated Barium Sulphate, or "Flake White," with Water containing enough Gum Arabic to prevent the immediate settling of the substance. Starch or Magnesium Carbonate may be used in a similar way. They must be reduced to palpable powders.

INDELIBLE INK FOR MARKING LINEN.—Add Caustic Alkali to a saturated solution of Corpous Chloride until no further precipitate forms; allow the precipitate to settle, draw off the supernatant liquid with a siphon and dissolve the hydrated copper oxide in the smallest quantity of Ammonia. It may be mixed with about 6 per cent of Gum Dextrine for use.

TO WRITE SECRET LETTERS.—Put five cents' worth Citrate of Potassa in an ounce vial of clear cold water. This forms an invisible fluid. Let it dissolve and you can use on paper of any color. Use quill pen in writing. When you wish the writing to become visible hold it to red hot stove.

BLACK COPYING INK OR WRITING FLUID.—Take two gallons of Rain Water, and put into it Gum Arabic one-fourth pound, Brown Sugar one pound, clean Copperas one-fourth pound, Powdered Nutgall three-fourths pound; mix, and shake occasionally for ten days, and strain; if needed sooner let it stand in an iron kettle until the strength is obtained. This ink will stand the action of the atmosphere for centuries if required.

TO MAKE RUBBER STAMP INK.—Dissolve Aniline in hot Glycerine, and strain while hot or warm.

COMMERCIAL WRITING INK.—Galls one ounce, Gum one-half ounce, Cloves one-half ounce, Sulphate of Iron, one-half ounce, Water eight ounces. Digest by frequent shaking till it has sufficient color. This is a good durable ink and will bear diluting.

TRAVELERS' INK.—White Blotting Paper is saturated with Aniline Black, and several sheets are pasted together, so as to form a thick pad. When required for use a small piece is torn off and covered with a little water. The black liquid which dissolves out is a good writing ink. A square inch of paper will produce enough ink to last for a considerable writing, and a few pads would be all that an exploring party need carry with them. As water is always available the ink is readily made. This is a perfectly original and new recipe. Any enterprising man can make a large income out of its manufacture.

INDELIBLE MARKING INK WITHOUT A PREPARATION.—Dissolve separately one ounce of Nitrate of Silver and one and one-half ounces of Sub-Carbonate of Soda (best washing soda) in rain water. Mix the solutions and collect and wash the precipitate in a filter; while still moist rub it up in a marble or hardwood mortar with three drachms of Tartaric Acid, add two ounces of Rain Water, mix six drachms White Sugar and ten drachms powdered Gum Arabic, one-half ounce Archill and Water to make up six ounces in measure. It should be put up in short drachm bottles and sold at twenty-five cents. This is the best ink for marking clothes that has ever been discovered. There is a fortune in this recipe, as a good marking ink is very salable.

INVISIBLE INK.—Sulphuric Acid one quart, Water twenty parts; mix together and write with a quill pen, which writing can be read only after heating it.

HORTICULTURAL INK.—Copper one part, dissolve in Nitric Acid ten parts and add Water ten parts; used to write on zinc or tin labels.

GOLD INK.—Honey and Gold Leaf equal parts, Turpentine until the Gold is reduced to the finest possible state of division, agitate with thirty parts Hot Water and allow it to settle. Decant the Water and repeat the washing several times; finally dry the Gold and mix it with a little Gum Water for use.

SILVER INK.—For silver ink the process is the same as gold, substituting Silver Leaf for the Gold leaf.

INDELIBLE INK FOR GLASS OR METAL.—Borax one ounce, Shellac two ounces, Water eighteen fluid ounces; boil in a covered vessel, add of thick Mucilage one ounce; triturate it with Levigated Indigo and Lamp Black q.s. to give it a good color. After two hours' repose decant from the dregs and bottle for use. It may be bronzed after being applied. Resists moisture, chlorine and gases.

BROWN INK.—A strong decoction of Catechu. The shade may be varied by the cautious addition of a little weak solution of bicromate of potash.

LUMINOUS INK.—Shines in the dark. Phosphorous one-half drachm, Oil Cinnamon one-half ounce; mix in a vial, cork tightly, heat it slowly until mixed. A letter written in this ink can only be read in a dark room, when the writing will have the appearance of a fire.

PASTE TO PRODUCE WHISKERS.—One ounce of Oil of Paricada, two ounces Southern Wood Bark, one ounce Dog's Lard. Fry over a slow fire until it forms a paste. Apply to the face once a day until the whiskers begin to grow.

TO CLEAN THE TEETH.—Castile Soap and Cigar Ashes applied with a soft rag is one of the best tooth preparations known.

TO MAKE THE HAIR SOFT AND GLOSSY.—One pint Alcohol, four ounces Castor Oil. Mix, and flavor with Bergamot. Apply frequently with the hands.

TO REMOVE FRECKLES.—Use Oxolate of Copper Ointment.

HAIR TONIC.—Sugar of Lead five grains, Sulphate Quinine two grains, Muriat of Ammonia one drachm, Glycerine six ounces, Distilled Water six ounces. Mix and apply two or three times per day.

HAIR DYES. NO. 1.—Distilled Water six ounces, Alcohol one ounce, Pyrogalic Acid one drachm. The Acid must be dissolved in the Alcohol before the water is added.

NO. 2.—Aqua Ammonia one ounce, Water one ounce, Nitrate of Silver two drachms. Dissolve the Silver in water and add the Ammonia. Cork tight and keep in a cool place.

NO. 3.—Water four ounces, Sulphate of Potash half ounce. Mix. To dye the hair or whiskers, have them free from dirt or soap suds. They should be a little damp. Add carefully No. 1, using care not to allow the dye to touch the skin. When somewhat dry apply No. 2; in about three minutes apply No. 3. Use care not to allow any of these preparations to touch the skin.

TO BEAUTIFY THE TEETH AND MAKE THE BREATH SMELL SWEET AND PLEASANT.—One ounce Chlorate of Lime in a pint of Soft Water, and let it stand 24 hours. Then pour off the clear water and add forty drops of Essence of Rose.

TO MAKE THE CHEEKS AND LIPS ROSY.—Use a little Red Carmine.

PERFUMERY.—Oils of Rosemary and Lemon each a half ounce, Bergamot and Lavender half drachm, Cinnamon four drops, Cloves and Rose each two drops, Alcohol one quart. Mix and let stand one week.

HAIR RESTORATIVE.—Sugar of Lead, Borax and Lac Sulphur each one ounce, Aqua Ammonia half ounce, Alcohol one gill. Mix and let stand 20 hours, then add Bay Rum one gill, fine Table Salt one tablespoonful, Soft Water three pints, Essence of Bergamot half ounce.

NEW YORK BARBER'S STAR HAIR OIL.—Castor Oil six and one-half pints, Alcohol one and one-half pints, Oil of Citronella one-half ounce, Lavender one-fourth ounce. Mix well, put in four ounce bottles, retail for 25 cents.

CELEBRATED MOTH AND FRECKLE LOTION.—For the skin and complexion; a great secret. Distill two handfuls Jessamine Flowers in a quart of Rose Water and a quart of Orange Water. Strain through porous paper and add a scruple of Musk and a scruple of Ambergris. Bottle and label. Splendid wash for the skin.

IMPERIAL ONGUENT FOR FORCING WHISKERS AND MUSTACHE TO GROW.—Made as follows: Two drachms of Benzoin Comp., two drachms Tincture of Cantharides, six ounces of Castor Oil, nine and one-fourth ounces Alcohol, one drachm Oil of Bergamot. Mix well, bottle and label. Apply the Onguent night and morning. Circulation should be stimulated with a rough towel.

CURLOLINE, FOR MAKING THE HAIR CURL.—One pound Olive Oil, one drachm Oil of Origanum, one and one-half drachms Oil of Rosemary. Mix well, bottle and label. Apply two or three times weekly. Will curl the straightest hair if not cut too short.

HAIR RESTORATIVE AND INVIGORATOR.—For a trifling cost. Sugar of Lead, Borax and Lac Sulphur of each one ounce, Aqua Ammonia one-half ounce, Alcohol one gill. mix and let stand for fourteen hours; then add Bay

Rum one gill, fine Table Salt one tablespoonful, Soft Water three pints, Essence of Bergamot one ounce. This preparation not only gives a beautiful gloss, but will cause hair to grow upon bald heads arising from all common causes, and turning gray hair to a dark color.

*Manner of Application.*—When the hair is thin or bald, make two applications daily, until this amount is used up. Work it into the roots of the hair with a soft brush or the ends of the fingers, rubbing well each time. For gray hair one application daily is sufficient.

JOCKEY CLUB.—Spirits of Wine five gallons, Orange Flower Water one gallon, Balsam of Peru four ounces, Essence of Bergamot eight ounces. Essence of Musk eight ounces, Essence of Cloves four ounces, Essence of Neroli two ounces. Mix.

LADIES' OWN.—Spirits of Wine one gallon, Otto of Roses twenty drops, Essence of Thyme one-half ounce, Essence of Neroli one-fourth ounce, Essence of Vanilla one-half ounce, Essence of Bergamot one-fourth ounce, Orange Flower Water six ounces.

UPPER TEN.—Spirits of Wine four quarts, Essence of Cedrat two drachms, Essence of Violets one-fourth ounce, Essence of Neroli one-half ounce, Otto of Roses twenty drops, Orange Flower Essence one ounce, Oil of Rosemary thirty drops, Oils of Bergamot and Neroli each one-half ounce.

# CHAPTER V.

## LIVE STOCK DEPARTMENT.

Each and Every Recipe in This Department Has Been Tested by the Most Eminent Veterinary Surgeons in the United States, and Pronounced by Them as the Best.

WOUNDS AND CUTS.—Take four ounces Lard, Beeswax four ounces, Resin three ounces, Vaseline four to six ounces. Melt these together and add Carbolic Acid half ounce. This is excellent.

COLIC.—Gum Camphor one ounce, Cayenne one ounce, Gum Myrrh one ounce, powdered Gum Quaial one ounce, Sassafras Bark one ounce, Spirits of Turpentine one ounce, Oil of Origanum one-quarter ounce, Oil Hemlock half ounce, Pulverized Opium half ounce, good alcohol two quarts. Mix and let stand ten to twelve days and filter. Dose from one to four teaspoonfuls in a pint of milk. Keep this on hand. It is the best colic cure known.

LINIMENT TO KILL PAIN.—One gallon Alcohol, one ounce Tincture Cayenne, two ounces Tincture Gum Camphor, two ounces Tincture Ammonia, one-half ounce Chloroform. Mix well and let stand twelve hours.

BEST CONDITION POWDERS.—Fenugreek, Cream of Tartar, Gentian, Sulphur, Saltpetre, Resin, Black Antimony and Ginger each two ounces, Cayenne Pepper one ounce. Pulverize and mix thoroughly. Dose, two tablespoonfuls once a day in feed.

BRITTLE AND CONTRACTED HOOFS.—Take Castor Oil, Barbadoes, Tar and Soft Soap. Equal parts of each. Melt all together and stir while cooling, and apply a little to the hoof three or four times a week.

CONTRACTED HOOF AND SORE FEET.—Take equal parts of Soft Fat, Yellow Wax, Linseed Oil, Venice Turpentine and Norway Tar; first melt the wax, then add the others, mixing thoroughly. Apply to the edge of the hair once a day.

CRACKED HEELS.—Tar eight ounces, Beeswax one ounce, Resin one ounce, Alum one ounce, Tallow one ounce, Sulphate of Iron one ounce, Carbolic Acid one drachm. Mix and boil over a slow fire. Skim off the filth and add two ounces of the scrapings of Sweet Elder.

EYE WATER.—White Vitriol and pure Saltpetre of each one scruple, pure soft water eight ounces. Mix. This should be applied to the inflamed lids three or four times a day, and if the inflammation does not lessen in one or two days it may be injected directly into the eye.

The writer has used this for his own eyes, reduced one-half with water, and dropped directly into the eye, which would cause the eye to smart considerably for about five minutes, when he should bathe the eye with cold water for a few minutes, and by repeating this three or four times a day, it has given the best of satisfaction. It does nicely, many times, to just close the eye and bathe the outside freely.

CURE FOR SWEENEY.—Alcohol and Spirits of Turpentine each eight ounces, Camphor Gum, pulverized Cantharides and Capsicum each one ounce, Oil of Spike three ounces. Mix. Bathe with hot iron.

FARCY.—Nitrate of Potash four ounces, Black Antimony two ounces, Sulphite of Soda one ounce, Elecampane two ounces. Mix. Dose, one tablespoonful once or twice a day.

FARCY AND GLANDERS.—Iodide of Potassium one and one-quarter drachms, Copperas one-half, Ginger one drachm, Gentian two drachms, powdered Gum Arabic and Syrup to form a ball; or, take one-half ounce Sulphite Soda, five grains powdered Cantharides. Mix, and give at night in cut feed for several weeks; give at the same time every morning and noon three drachms powdered Gentian, two drachms powdered Blue Vitriol, give the medicines for a long time; feed well. This is the best treatment that can be given for this disease.

WOLF'S LINIMENT.—One quart Alcohol, two ounces Tincture Arnica, one ounce Oil Hemlock, one ounce Oil of Spike. Mix well and let stand twenty-four hours. This will cure any burn, scald, bruise, sprain or any like ailment; also aches and pains of all kinds. Apply by wetting a flannel cloth and wrapping it around the diseased parts.

CUTS, WOUNDS AND SORES.—Take of Lard four ounces, Beeswax four ounces, Resin two ounces, Carbolic Acid one-quarter ounce. Mix the first three and melt, add Carbolic Acid, stirring until cool. This is excellent for man as well as beast.

FOR POLL EVIL.—Rock Salt one ounce, Blue Vitriol one ounce, Copperas one-half ounce. Pulverize and mix well. Fill a goose quill with the powder and push to the bottom of the pipe. Have a stick at the top of the quill and push the powder out of the quill, leaving it at the bottom of the pipe. Repeat in four days, and in two or three days you can remove the pipe without any trouble.

CURE FOR SCRATCHES.—Sweet Oil three ounces, Borax one ounce, Sugar of Lead one ounce. Mix and apply twice daily after washing thoroughly with castile soap, giving time for legs to dry.

GREAT ARABIAN HEAVE REMEDY.—Give your horse a teaspoonful of Lobelia once a day for a week and then once a week, and you will hardly know he ever had the heaves. Try it.

BOTS.—Take new Milk two quarts, Syrup one quart, mix and give the whole, and in fifteen or twenty minutes after give two quarts of warm, strong Sage tea; half an hour after the tea give one quart of raw Linseed Oil, or if the Oil cannot be had give Lard instead.

DIURETICS.—Take Balsam Copaiba two ounces, Sweet Spirits of Nitre three ounces, Spirits of Turpentine two ounces, Oil of Juniper two ounces, Tincture of Camphor two ounces. Mix; shake the bottle before pouring the medicine. Dose for adult horse, two tablespoonfuls in a pint of milk, repeated every four to six hours, if necessary. This is a reliable preparation for kidney difficulties.

FOUNDER.—Vinegar three pints, Capsicum one-half drachm, Tincture of Aconite Root fifteen drops. Mix and boil down to one quart; when cool give it as a drench. Blanket the horse well; after the horse has perspired for an hour or more, give one quart of raw Linseed Oil. This treatment will be found good for horses foundered by eating too much grain.

MANGE.—Oil Tar one ounce, Lac Sulphur one and one-half ounces, Whale Oil two ounces. Mix. Rub a little on the skin wherever the disease appears, and continue daily for a week, then wash off with castile soap and warm water.

POLL EVIL AND FISTULA.—Tincture of Opium one drachm, Potash two drachms, Water one ounce; mix, and when dissolved inject into the pipes with a small syringe, having cleansed the sore with soap-suds; repeat every two days until pipes are completely destroyed.

CONDITION POWDER.—Take Antimony Crude one ounce, Lobelia gr. one ounce, Ginger two ounces, Sulphur Flour three ounces, Berberry gr. one ounce, Cream Tartar four ounces, Saltpetre Flour four ounces; well mixed. Dose, one tablespoonful each day in wet feed. Best in the market; will sell well.

FOR BONE SPAVIN.—Hog's Lard half pint, best Oil Origanum one and a half ounces, Oil Cajeput two ounces, pulverized Cantharides half ounce.

Mix, and apply each morning for four mornings, heating it in with hot iron each time, then discontinue its use for three days, after which use as before for five mornings. Wait about eight or ten days and if not gone repeat as before.

ARABIAN HORSE TAMER'S SECRET.—Take Oil of Cummin, Oil of Rhodium and Horse Castor. Keep separate in air-tight bottles. Rub a little of the Oil of Cummin on your hand and approach the horse on the windward side, so that he can smell the Cummin. The horse will then let you come up to him without trouble. Rub your hand gently on the horse's nose, getting a little oil on it. He will then follow you. Give him a little of the Castor on a piece of Loaf Sugar or Apple; get a few drops of the Rhodium on his tongue, and he is your servant. He will follow you like a pet dog.

CURE FOR SPAVIN AND RINGBONE.—Cantharides one ounce, Mercurial Ointment half ounce, Corrosive Sublimate a half drachm, Turpentine one and a half ounces, Tincture Iodine one ounce, Gum Euphorbium four ounces. Mix well with one pound of Lard. For spavin or ringbone, cut the hair away and grease the part well with the ointment, rubbing it in well. In two days grease the parts with Lard; wash it off in two days more, and again apply the ointment. So continue until a cure is effected, which will be in a short time. For bog Spavin, wind gall, curb or splint, apply the ointment every six days.

JOCKEY TRICKS.—How to make a horse appear as though he was badly foundered.—Take a fine wire and fasten it tightly around the fetlock, between the foot and the heel, and smooth the hair over it. In twenty minutes the horse will show lameness. Do not leave it on over nine hours. To make a horse lame.—Take a single hair from its tail, put it through the eye of a needle, then lift the front leg and press the skin between the outer and middle tendon or cord, and shove the needle through, cut off the hair each side and let down the foot. The horse will go lame in twenty minutes. How to make a horse stand by his food and not take it.—Grease the front teeth and the roof of the mouth with common beef tallow, and he will not eat until you wash it out. This, in conjunction with the above, will consummate a complete founder. How to cure a horse from the crib or sucking wind.—Saw between the upper teeth to the gums. How to put a young countenance on a horse.—Make a small incision in the sunken place over the eye, insert the point of a goose quill and blow it up; close the external wound with a thread, and it is done. To cover up the heaves.—Drench the horse with one-fourth pound of common bird-shot, and he will not heave until they pass through him. To make a horse appear as if he had the glanders.—Melt four ounces fresh Butter and pour into his ear. To distinguish between glanders and distemper.—The discharge from the nose in glanders will sink in water; in distemper it floats. How to make a true pulling horse balk.—Take Tincture of Cantharides one ounce, and Corrosive Sublimate one drachm; mix and bathe his shoulder at night. How to serve a horse that is lame.—Make a small incision about half way from the knee to the joint on the outside of the leg, and at the back part of the shin bone you will find a small, white tendon or cord; cut it off and close the external wound with a stitch, and he will walk off on the hardest pavement and not limp a particle.

**HOW TO TELL THE AGE OF A HORSE.**—The safest way of determining the age of a horse is by the appearance of the teeth, which undergo certain changes in the course of years.

Eight to fourteen days after birth, the first middle nippers of the set of milk teeth are cut; four to six weeks afterwards the pair next to them, and finally, after six or eight months, the last.

All these milk teeth have a well defined body and neck, and a slender fang, and on their front surface grooves or furrows, which disappear from the middle nippers at the end of one year, from the next pair in two years, and from the incisive teeth (cutters) in three years.

At the age of two the nippers become loose and fall out, in their places appear two permanent teeth, with deep, black cavities, and full, sharp edges.

At the age of three, the next pair fall out.

At four years old, the corner teeth fall out.

At five years old, the horse has his permanent set of teeth.

The teeth grow in length as the horse advances in years, but at the same time his teeth are worn away by use about one-twelfth of an inch every year, so that the black cavities of the center nippers below disappear in the sixth year, those of the next pair in the seventh year, and those of the corner teeth in the eighth year. Also the outer corner of upper and lower jaw just meet at eight years of age.

At nine years old, cups leave the two center nippers above, and each of the two upper corner teeth has a little sharp protrusion at the extreme outer corner.

At the age of ten the cups disappear from the adjoining teeth.

At the age of eleven, the cups disappear from the corner teeth above, and are only indicated by brownish spots.

The oval form becomes broader, and changes, from the twelfth to the sixteenth year, more and more into a triangular form, and the teeth lose, finally, with the twentieth year, all regularity. There is nothing remaining in the teeth that can afterwards clearly show the age of the horse, or justify the most experienced examiner in giving a positive opinion.

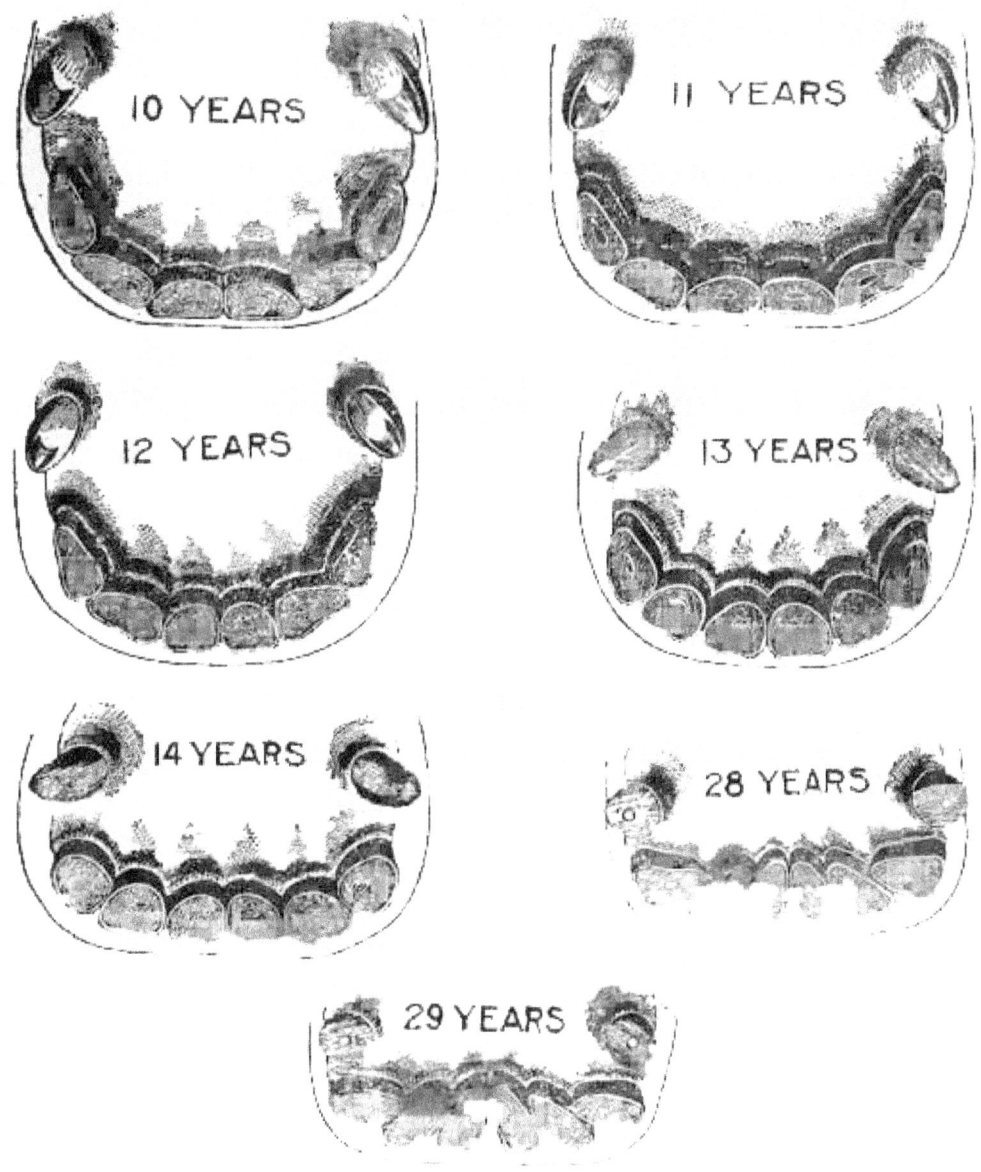

The tushes, or canine teeth, conical in shape, with a sharp point, and curved, are cut between the third and fourth year, their points become more and more rounded until the ninth year, and after that, more and more dull in the course of years, and lose, finally, all regular shape. Mares seldom have tusks; if any, they are very faintly indicated.

Frequent reference to the chart for telling the horse's age will thoroughly acquaint one with this valuable bit of knowledge.

**AGE OF SHEEP AND GOATS.**—At one year old they have eight front teeth of uniform size. At two years the two middle ones are supplanted by two large ones. At three a small tooth appears on each side. At four there are six large teeth. At five all the front teeth are large, and at six all begin to get worn.

**AGE OF CATTLE.**—A cow's horn is supposed to furnish a correct indication of the age of the animal, but this is not always true. For ordinary purposes, however, the following will be found approximately correct: At two years of age a circle of thicker matter begins to form on the animal's horns, which becomes clearly defined at three years of age, when another circle begins to form, and an additional circle every year thereafter. The cow's age then can be determined by adding two to the number of circles. The rings on a bull's horns do not show themselves until he is five years old—so in the case of a bull five must be added to the number of rings. Unless the rings are clear and distinct these rules will not apply. Besides, dishonest dealers sometimes file off some of the rings of old cattle.

# CHAPTER VI.

## HOG DEPARTMENT.

### THE DISPOSITION AND CHARACTER OF THE HOG.

In all histories of animals, the hog stands a natural phenomenon, and alone in relation to his appetite and physical constitution. The hog is the only kind of animal known to man that can feed on any kind of food. The stomach of the hog is adapted both to flesh and grass, which is not the case with any other animal in all the history of animals. Another peculiarity of his nature is his great ferociousness; perhaps the hog is more valiant than any animal known. The ferocious and warlike disposition (perhaps) is one among the reasons of this animal's great health. There are very few diseases among animals that the hog is subject to; in fact, it (the Cholera) is the only disease to be greatly feared among that order of animals; and as this great and valuable remedy is found and demonstrated beyond the shadow of a doubt, the farmer may go on raising and feeding his hogs with the full assurance that his labors will not be lost. He can improve his hogs with confidence and assurance that health and prosperity will be the rich reward of his labors.

There is more money made in the culture and growing of hogs than any animal in the known world; notwithstanding the great loss by Cholera, there is no one but what will say amen to this fact. Even Boone County loses $100,000.00 worth of hogs with the Cholera, annually. There are 114 counties in the State of Missouri. Now make the calculation of the great saving of money by this invaluable discovery for the prevention and cure of the above disease. We see that if all farmers and traders in hogs had this book, and carried out its instructions, it would save $11,400,000.00 for the State of Missouri, which amount would soon enable Missouri or any other State that observes this book's instructions to be the richest State in the Union.

There is no farmer but that will become wealthy if he uses economy, industry and has the Stephen's Remedy for Hog Cholera.

## SYMPTOMS OF THE DISEASE, HOG CHOLERA.

1st. Gentleness and sluggishness.

2d. You will see the hog moving around with his nose close to the ground, with a kind of a forced cough, hair looking dead and kind of a reddish color; then they quit eating and soon die. These symptoms are generally of a slow progress, but certain death if Stephen's Cholera Remedy is not used. These symptoms are set forth both in dry and purging Hog Cholera. On the first appearance, this disease is more fatal, from the fact that nature teaches the brute, by unlearned laws, natural medical aid; but this disease is so powerful and destructive there is something more necessary than the animal can generally get at.

We now propose to give the cause and the whole cause of the fearful disease caused Hog Cholera: The system of both man and brute is made up and composed of a living animalcule so small that it cannot be discovered with the eye, it being so delicate; but, by the use of the microscope, it can be readily seen and realized. In good health, with this animal, this animalcule is the life and spirit of the hog, causing the functions throughout the whole system to perform nature's intended designs—regular digestion, and a perfect circulation throughout the whole animal nature; but when this valuable animal is ranging in certain localities where he has no resort to certain material, the system becomes of an impure character, and this delicate animalcule commanding a rapid growth, feeds upon the nutriment of the body of the hogs and consequently destroys life without a counteracting remedy of speedy effect. The liver is the seat of worms or animalcule; it is also the king or main spring of digestion of both man and beast; when the hog begins to droop, the worm is rapidly growing; and, without something to destroy this worm, the hog will die. In certain localities the hog never has this disease.

Now, this is full and ample evidence that it is the locality in relation to feed that keeps this fearful disease from the hog. In my travels I have observed, the localities and health of this valuable animal depends on what range or food he gets. The Author, having traveled through different countries and localities, observing at the same time the health of this animal, gave rise to this great discovery as a perfect remedy for health. This remedy will both prevent and cure this disease, when the disease has not too strong a hold, and the liver and blood fevered too much by the worm. The liver, being the seat of digestion, must not be disturbed; if its digestion is disturbed, secretions are located—the system depending on the liver as the clock or watch depends on its mainspring for time; therefore, knowing the disease and remedy, end experiencing the facts, the Author is fully satisfied that his remedy, both as a preventative and cure, is all that it claims to be, and is undoubtedly the most valuable discovery for the health of the swine that has ever been known or found out.

The reasons and cause of Hog Cholera having been explained, the Author now proposes to give the

### PREVENTION AND CURE OF HOG CHOLERA.

We are aware of the fact that the talent, ingenuity and skill of man has been employed in searching out some remedy as a preventative and cure for this lamentable disease; and there have been some preventions used that have been valuable in that direction. For instance, the simple article called ashes is a healthy article for stock, which many people use, but it never cured one case of Cholera. I have no doubt but it has been beneficial for the general health of hogs. Of all remedies, simple ones when they will cure are the best; and this remedy is as simple and as easily used as it is possible in the use of any remedy.

The effective remedy is simply old lime and sand, with arsenic. Now, I am aware that the nature of man is to look for some great and unknown article as a remedy for such a great curse as Hog Cholera; but, considering the cause of the disease being the animalcule, reader, you see that it requires something to prevent the excess, or destroy the increase of this minute animal. Now, we see readily that the Old Lime, Sand and Arsenic does the work without a doubt, and the hog is healthy and clear of disease.

Now, reader, you have the remedy; the next thing is how to use it.

In the first place drive your wagon to some sandbar and haul a wagon load of sand; throw it out where you feed your hogs; to one wagon load of sand, put one bushel of old slacked lime; throw your feed on that for your hogs, and about every three months replenish with the same. If your hogs have the Cholera, separate the sick from the well ones, and have a trough, and put some of the sand and lime in it, with about one-half of a thimbleful of arsenic to the hog; then pour some rich slop on this preparation so that the hogs will eat it; milk would be preferable if you have it. This preparation once every other day will soon have your hogs healthy and sound; it destroys the worms, then the hog is all right. To your healthy hogs give one-half thimbleful of arsenic in slop to every hog, once per month. This is all the arsenic you must use; you must not mix the arsenic with the lime and sand, or the hog may not get it.

After using this remedy, your hogs that are not yet complaining with Cholera will never take it; you may rely on it. I have tried this valuable remedy until I am perfectly satisfied; where the Cholera was killing out the gang every day, it put a stop to it at once; and not only for myself, but many others under my notice. I have never seen Cholera bother hogs, where this Stephen's Remedy was used as above stated. You will ask, what is to be done where pigs have it? In answer to that, reader, just get a trough and put in the remedy, and pour the slop to their mother, and the milk will be just as effective to the pigs as the remedy is with the sow.

This Stephen's Remedy for Hog Cholera, if studied and observed, will be worth from $100.00 to $1,000.00 to every farmer or hog trader, where Cholera has ever been; and there is no trouble or expense to have the benefit of it. This very little book is worth its weight in gold. The countries where they have no Hog Cholera are rocky and hilly, sandy and limy, where the

C. A. Bogardus

hog can get this remedy, and Providence has so taught the animal that nature dictates to him the remedy. See the dog, when he is sick, he knows how to take an emetic, vomit, and get well; so it is with the hog, if he can find this remedy he hardly ever takes Cholera.

In addition to those cures as a prevention of the disease, use Asafetida, as follows: Cut in small pieces about one ounce; melt it in water or grease, pour it in rich slop. Feed it to about ten hogs, once per week in Hog Cholera season, more or less according to number of hogs. If you will keep up these remedies your swine will keep healthy. Keep the sick ones and well ones separate. If you have clover keep the sick ones on it, it is healthy for hogs.

## ON TREATMENT.

A little further advice concerning the treatment of hogs when penned for fattening; hogs should be penned on rolling ground if possible; they fatten better and consume less corn; they should be salted twice a week. The way to salt is as follows: If there is no decaying stump in the pen, haul a rotten log and pour salt on it, and the hogs will use all the salt and waste none; and the demands of nature will have them use just enough and no more; this preparation will save 2½ bushels of corn to every hog, which is $1.00—quite an item where you have a large pen of hogs. Salt your stock hogs in the same way. When you have used Stephen's Remedies one year, you would not be without this knowledge for any small amount, for your hogs will be healthy and prosperous. If the reader has only one hog per year, it will pay him to buy this book in relation to the breed of hogs. I don't know that I could enlighten you on this subject, for the world's attention is directed to that information, and perhaps, reader, you are as well posted on that subject as your humble writer. For the western country, as a hardy and profitable stock of thrifty hogs, the Berkshire mixed or crossed with the Poland China, would be my choice, but every man has his own notions concerning the breed of his stock. The main point is to keep them healthy. Please fathom these instructions, which will cost you no more hard labor.

Now, reader, the Author has endeavored, in his plain and simple manner, and in as few words as possible, to explain the cause of Hog Cholera, its effects, symptoms, and its cure and prevention, which have been demonstrated by the Author, and not only by him but by divers others under his instruction.

Before the Author wrote this book, he sold these receipts at from $10.00 to $50.00; but seeing the great loss of labor and perplexity in relation to Hog Cholera, and the pressing necessity throughout our land, alone induced the Author of this work to write a book and set such a low price on it as to enable every poor widow, that has even a pet pig, to be in possession of one as a security for its health.

## ADVICE TO THE YOUNG MAN.

When the young man leaves his father's home to plan out his course as a farmer it is very necessary for him to observe two grand points:

1st. To so live, act and speak, as the Apostle Paul says, "void of offense both to God and man;" and in these words there is a world of thought. This constitutes our noblest characters in this life and the life to come.

2nd. In relation to finance, or making and saving of money. Purchase a good farm, just as much land as you can cultivate well, and no more; don't have one surplus acre; don't do like some people, raise every kind of stock and never have anything for market; but when you raise hogs, raise nothing else for market but hogs; and raise all you can fatten—that is, all you can raise corn to make fat; and by this rule to have one or two car loads for sale every fall; you will become wealthy if you live to be old.

In relation to managing your fields, be sure not to exhaust your soil; if you are in timber land, sow wheat every other year on your corn-fields; this will keep your land constantly improving from ordinary land to rich land. If you live in prairie country where your wheat will not pay, never sow oats unless you let your hogs take them before cutting. Always have one clover field for your hogs to run on in the hard months of summer and fall.

Now, reader, in conclusion, I will give you certificates of the most prominent men in our vicinity, who tried and experienced the Stephen's Hog Cholera Remedy, and became convinced of its great value and benefit to man; and that all men may have confidence and rely on this remedy as a fact, these men have gone before the Justice of the Peace and sworn to the facts as they exist. You will see their certificates on the following pages.

Now, reader, hoping we may both be greatly benefited by this little work, I bid you God speed. Good-bye.

---

### HOG CHOLERA.

This is to certify that I bought one of Dr. J. H. Stephen's Hog Cholera books in 1880, when my hogs were dying with that disease. I went home and followed the directions of the book. I cured my hogs and prevented the rest from having the disease. I here state I have followed Dr. Stephen's book's directions for fifteen years, feeding and raising hogs, with Cholera around me, and have kept my hogs healthy ever since. You need not be afraid of Hog Cholera if you have one of the books. The remedy will not cost more than one dollar a year for one hundred hogs. No one that has hogs can afford to do without it. I was living in Monroe county when I bought the book. I am now living in Brunswick, Chariton county, Mo., with Hog Cholera all around me. I am not afraid of it. If you doubt this, write to me.

REUBEN YOUNG.

Witness, B. G. YOUNG.
October 15, 1895.

## A VALUABLE DISCOVERY FOR EVERYBODY.

In 1870 my hogs, and many of those of my neighbors, died with Hog Cholera; it also broke out again in '71. Dr. Stephens, of Centralia, discovered a never failing cure for Hog Cholera. I used his remedy, it being no expense or trouble, and I never lost a hog, while every one of my neighbors lost a large portion of their hogs by disease. My hogs running with them, I am satisfied that I would have lost them, had it not been for this great remedy of Stephens, that I used. I am satisfied that this remedy will either cure or prevent Hog Cholera in any case. I am an old farmer, and would not be without this sure remedy for any reasonable sum of money. I conscientiously and unhesitatingly advise every farmer to not fail to get at least a farm right, and save your hogs from that dreadful destructive disease; for the remedy will cure and prevent Hog Cholera in any case. I have experienced this fact, and the benefit of it is the reason I set so high a value on it. I am a sojourner near Cairo, Randolph county, Mo. Was born in Kentucky and emigrated to Missouri in an early day.

THOMAS PATRICK.

June 24, 1872.

## VALUABLE NOTICE.

I hereby state a valuable fact. My hogs were dying with Cholera in the fall of 1871; I offered the lot for a certain sum of money. They were dying every day with Hog Cholera, in Boone County. I finally offered them for a mere nominal sum, not being one-fifth part of the value of the hogs, had not the Cholera been among them, and they dying every day. Dr. J. H. Stephens of Centralia, Mo., said he could cure them, and Mr. R. E. Edwards, of Centralia, Mo., having faith in Dr. Stephens, bought the hogs. To my own knowledge, the hogs were cured and fatted up, and made well; and I say for the benefit of the public, that I believe that Dr. Stephens can either cure or prevent Hog Cholera on any man's farm. I advise all farmers to get his great and valuable remedy; it may save you thousands of dollars.

Given under my hand this June 22nd, 1872. This is for no benefit of mine, but alone for the benefit of the public. This is a fact.

E. T. BENNETT,
Trustee of the M.E. Church,
Centralia.

Subscribed and sworn to before me on this 22nd day of June, 1872.

J. M. WEST, J.P.

---

## TO ALL MY FRIENDS, AND THEN TO STRANGERS.

Centralia, Boone Co., July 3, 1872.

Dr. Stephens, of this place, I believe, has discovered at last the great remedy both to cure and to prevent Hog Cholera. This disease has made its ravages among hogs in every State like cholera among men, but I hope and believe from experience, that Dr. Stephens has, after all the remedies have been tried, discovered the great and only reliable remedy, I am satisfied from theory and experience that his remedy will both cure and prevent Hog Cholera. I bought a lot of hogs, every one of which had the Cholera, on the faith that Dr. Stephens would cure them. I bought the hogs of E. T. Bennett, living in our town. They were dying every day, and I bought them at a mere nominal sum, it not being, perhaps, one-fifth or sixth part of the value of said hogs. I called on Dr. Stephens, and he instructed me what to do. The remedy cost me but a trifle and I cured every one, and my hogs fattened and did well—other hogs dying all over town—mine cured sound and remained healthy. I am not afraid of Hog Cholera any more; at least I am satisfied I can cure it with Dr. Stephens' great remedy. This remedy I never before heard of for Hog Cholera; but I have experienced the fact. The great value is, it costs you, to prevent 1,000 hogs from having it one year with three hours' labor, but $1.00. My advice is, don't fail to obtain this valuable remedy at any cost. This is a fact that I believe is worth more, and a greater saver of money to the United States than any discovery that has been made in the 19th century.

R. F. EDWARDS,
Sup't. of the M.E. Sunday School, Centralia, Mo.

Subscribed and sworn to before me, this 3rd day of July, 1872.
JAMES M. WEST, J.P.

# CHAPTER VII.

## POULTRY DEPARTMENT.

### THE TREATMENT OF FOWLS.

In the rearing of poultry for profit it may safely be stated that dry, well-aired, warm poultry houses are necessary.

To keep fowls in poorly ventilated, damp, cold quarters is a waste of time and money, as nearly all diseases of fowls are traceable to improperly kept poultry houses.

It may also be stated that 99 per cent of the sickness in fowls has its origin in filth, hence cleanliness is essential in raising good poultry.

The hen house should be cleaned as often as the barn.

## DISEASES OF FOWLS AND HOW TO TREAT THEM.

**Apoplexy.**—This disease is usually caused by over feeding in confined quarters. The bird may be noticed moping for some days, but usually the trouble is not noticed until the bird falls and dies with hardly a struggle.

**Remedy.**—Open the largest of the veins under the wing, press on the vein between the opening and the body until the blood flows freely.

**Vertigo.**—Like apoplexy, is caused by over feeding and lack of exercise. The fowl runs in a circle with but partial control of the limbs.

**Remedy.**—Hold the head of the bird under a stream of cold water. Give ten grains of jalap and reduce the amount of feed.

**Crop-Bound.**—Is caused by irregular feeding. A hungry bird fills his crop to such a degree that the contents, when moistened, becomes a dense compact mass.

**Remedy.**—Puncture the upper part of the crop, loosen the mass by degrees, with a blunt instrument. If the incision is large, sew up the slit and feed the bird soft food for ten days.

**Diarrhoea.**—Remedy.—Five grains powdered chalk, 5 grains turkey rhubarb, 5 grains cayenne pepper.

**Roup.**—This is a very contagious disease. The well fowls should immediately be separated from the sick ones, and the old quarters thoroughly disinfected. Use the following remedy. One-half ounce balsam copaiba, one-quarter ounce liquorice powder, one-half drachm piperine. This is enough for thirty doses. Enclose each dose in a small capsule; give two or three doses per day. If this does not furnish relief in two days, kill the fowl and burn or bury it.

The symptoms of this disease are first, a thick opaque and peculiarly offensive smelling discharge from the nostrils. Froth appears at the inner corner of the eyes, the lids swell and often the eyes are entirely closed; the sides of the face become much swollen, and the bird rapidly declines and dies.

**Gapes.**—Is caused by parasitic worms in the wind pipe, or from a small tick-like parasite lodged on the head of the chicken when between two and four months old. Examine the head of the bird, with a pocket lens, and if the parasite is found, destroy them with the following: One ounce mercurial ointment, one-half ounce petroleum (crude), one-half ounce flower of sulphur. Mix by heating, and apply when just warm.

When gapes is caused by worms in the wind pipe, use spirits of turpentine, it is applied by dipping the end of a feather in the turpentine, then inserting it in the bird's mouth at the root of the tongue; generally one operation is all that is required.

To prevent and cure chicken cholera, renovate the coops thoroughly then saturate the apartments with kerosene oil. Then grease the chicken under the wings and wherever the feathers are off, use the formula mentioned for gapes when caused by parasite (on the head), repeat the greasing process in two weeks, then once a month until the time of heavy frost in the fall.

The following is an elegant internal treatment. Dissolve four ounces of hyposulphate of soda in one gallon of water and add corn meal to make a heavy dough, and give an ordinary feed of this twice a day for six days, and then once a week through the summer months. In severe cases give one teaspoonful of the water (without meal) three or four times a day until out of danger. This is the best known remedy for chicken cholera.

**Poultry Lousiness.**—Appears only in poorly kept fowls. Sprinkle the fowls and nests with Scotch snuff or flower of sulphur. In addition thoroughly cleanse the hen house and coop with a solution of four pounds of potash to a gallon of water or with strong soap suds.

# CHAPTER VIII.

## CHEMICAL DEPARTMENT.

HOW TO IMITATE GOLD.—Take the following metals and melt them in a covered crucible; sixteen ounces Virgin Platina, twenty-four ounces pure copper.

SILVER.—Forty ounces Nickel, twenty ounces Copper, thirty ounces Block Tin.

ARTIFICIAL GOLD.—Sixteen parts of Virgin Platina and seven parts Copper and one of Zinc. Put these in a crucible with powdered charcoal, and melt them together till the whole forms a mass, and are thoroughly incorporated together. This also makes a gold of extraordinary beauty and value. It is not possible by any tests that chemists know of to distinguish it from pure virgin gold. All I ask of men is to use it for good and lawful purposes, for the knowledge that I here give you will bring you a rich and permanent reward without using it for unlawful purposes.

MANHEIM, OR JEWELER'S GOLD.—Three parts of Copper, one part of Zinc, and one part of Block Tin. If these are pure and melted in a covered crucible containing charcoal, the resemblance will be so good the best judges cannot tell it from pure gold without analyzing it.

BEST PINCHBACK GOLD.—Five ounces of pure Copper and one ounce of Zinc. This makes gold so good in appearance that a great deal of deception by its use in the way of watches and jewelry has been successfully practiced for several hundred years back.

SILVER FLUID.—For silvering brass and copper articles of every description.—Take an ounce of precipitated Silver to half an ounce of Cyanate of Potash and quarter of an ounce of Hyper Sulphate of Soda. Put all into a quart of water, add a little whitening and shake before using. Apply with a soft rag. This knowledge alone is worth one hundred dollars.

ORIGINAL AND GENUINE SILVER PLATING.—Galvanism Simplified.—Dissolve one ounce of Nitrate of Silver in Crystal in twelve ounces of soft water. Then dissolve in the water two ounces of Cyanate of Potash. Shake the whole together and let it stand until it becomes clear. Have ready some half-ounce vials, and fill them half full with Paris White or fine Whiting, then fill up the bottles with the liquid, and it is ready for use. The Whiting does not increase the coating power; it only helps to clean the articles and to save the silver fluid by half filling the bottles. The above quantity of materials will only cost about $1.50, so that the fluid will only cost about three cents a bottle.

POWDER FOR CLEANING AND POLISHING TIN, BRITANNIA AND BRASSWARE.—Take one-half pound ground Pumice Stone and one-quarter pound Red Chalk, mix them evenly together. This is for tin brass. For silver and fine ware, take one-half pound Red Chalk, and one-quarter pound Pumice Stone, mix evenly; use these articles dry with a piece of wash leather. It is one of the best cleaning powders ever invented, and very valuable.

SILVER POLISH FOR TIN, BRASS AND METALLIC ARTICLES.—Quicksilver, Tinfoil or Rottenstone, equal parts, all pulverized together. Roll up in balls, show as you go, and sell for 10 cents a ball.

ANOTHER.—Fine.—Four pounds Whiting, one-quarter ounce Oxalic Acid, one-half ounce Cream Tartar. Stir all together, then add slowly three ounces Mercury stirring briskly all the time so it will mix. This is good, 25 cents a ball.

KANGAROO CEMENT.—Rubber one ounce, pack tightly as possible in a bottle and cover it with Bi-Sulphate of Carbon. When the rubber is dissolved you will have the best cement in the world. There is a fortune in this to an energetic man, as it sells at 25 cents a drachm; and costs but little to make it. This is the cement used by shoemakers to put invisible patches on shoes.

HOW TO EAT FIRE.—Anoint your tongue with liquid Storax, and you may put hot iron or fire coals into your mouth, and without burning you. This is a very dangerous trick to be done, and those who practice it ought to use all means they can to prevent danger. We never saw one of those fire-eaters that had a good complexion.

IMITATION SILVER.—Eleven ounces refined Nickel, two ounces Metallic Bismuth. Melt the composition three times, and pour them out in ley. The third time, when melting, add two ounces of pure silver.

IMITATION GOLD.—Four ounces of Platina, three ounces of Silver, one ounce of Copper.

OROIDE GOLD.—The best article is made by compounding four parts pure Copper, one and three-fourths part pure Zinc, one-fourth part Magnesia, one-tenth part Sal-Ammoniac, one-twelfth part Quick Lime, and one part Cream Tartar. Melt the Copper first, then add as rapidly as possible the other articles in the order named.

HOW TO INCREASE THE WEIGHT OF GOLD.—Take your bar of Gold and rub it long and carefully with thin Silver, until the Gold absorbs the quantity of Silver that you require. Then prepare a strong solution of Brimstone and Quicklime. Now put the Gold into a vessel with a wide mouth. Now let them boil until the Gold attains the right color, and you have it, but do not use this knowledge for an ill purpose.

MASON'S FROZEN PERFUME.—This perfume is in a solid, transparent form, and by rubbing on the handkerchief it imparts an exquisite perfume; by carrying it in the pocket it perfumes the entire wearing apparel; by keeping it in a drawer or box all articles therein obtain the benefits of this perfume.

Solidified perfumes are superior to all liquid, as they cannot spill or waste in any manner, but will last for years. Perhaps no article of luxury had such a sale as this, and as the sales have steadily increased since its introduction, no other proof of its excellence is needed.

FREEZING MIXTURE.—Take four parts Nitric Acid, six parts Nitrate Ammonia, and nine parts phosphate of Soda. Having first prepared a vessel of galvanized iron four inches wide, twenty-four inches long, and twelve inches deep, have it a little wider at the top than at the bottom. Now make another vessel eight inches wide, twenty-eight inches long and fourteen inches high. Put the small vessel inside the larger one, fill the small one nearly full of as cool water as you can procure, put the freezing mixture in the large vessel around the smaller one, set this in as cool a place as possible. If you will have a faucet at the lower edge of the larger vessel and first fill the large vessel with the following it will greatly assist in freezing. Equal parts of Sal-Ammonia and Nitre dissolved in its own weight of water. In ten to fifteen minutes pour this off and put in the freezing mixture.

NOTE.—I have used the above description of a vessel to give you an idea of how to operate. Any sized vessel made in the same proportion will work as well.

IMPROVED TROY STARCH ENAMEL.—Melt five pounds of Refined Paraffine Wax in a tin boiler or pan over a slow fire; use care in melting. When melted remove the vessel from the fire and add 200 drops of Oil of Citronelli. Take some new round tin pie pans, and oil them with sweet oil as you would for pie baking, but do not use lard. Put these pans on a level table, and pour in enough of the hot wax to make a depth in each pan equal to about the thickness of one-eighth of an inch. While hot, glance over the pans to see that they are level. As this is very essential, please remember it. If the pans are not level, the cakes will be all thicknesses, which should not be so. Then let them cool, but not too fast. Watch them closely, and have a tin stamp ready to stamp the cakes out about the size of an ordinary candy lozenge. This stamp should be about eight inches long, larger at the top than at the bottom, so that the cakes can pass up through the stamp as you are cutting them out of the pans. Lay the cakes in another pan to cool. Before they become very hard, separate them from each other; if not, it will be difficult to do so when they become very hard. Do not neglect this. Have boxes made at any paper box maker's in any large city. They cost about from one to two cents each; sliding boxes are the best. Have your labels printed, and commence business at once. Put 24 to 30 cakes in each box, and retail for 25 cents.

Wholesale for $1.50 per dozen.

*Directions for Use.*—To a pint of boiling starch stir in one cake or tablet. This gives an excellent lustre to linen or muslin, and imparts a splendid perfume to the clothes, and makes the iron pass very smoothly over the surface. It requires but half the ordinary labor to do an ironing. It is admired by every lady. It prevents the iron from adhering to the surface, and the clothes remain clean and neat much longer than by any other method.

BRILLIANT SELF-SHINING STOVE POLISH.—This is one of the greatest inventions of the age. It has been the result of a large amount of study on the part of the inventor to perfect a polish that would work easily and satisfactorily in a perfect dry state, thereby obviating the disagreeable task of mixing and preparing. A good stove polish is an absolute necessity in every family. It is only a question, then, of offering the best to make a sale. To prove that this polish is the best is an easy task. All you have to do is to have a box open and a piece of rag to begin operations. You now approach the stove and apply the polish. The result will be so startlingly beautiful that no further words will be necessary. If the stove is not convenient, anything will do to experiment with. You can produce on a piece of wood, a scrap of paper or a potato, a lustre equal to a burnished mirror.

Now make the following points just as strong as you can:

That this polish requires no water or mixing like the various cake or powder polishes. 2. That it is self-shining and no labor is required. 3. That no dust or smell of any kind rises from its use. And, lastly, that it has no equal in the world.

RECIPE.—Take Plumbago (Black Lead) finely pulverized, and put in two ounce wood boxes, nicely labeled, and sell for ten or fifteen cents a box. Wholesale to stores and agents at $6.00 a hundred. Costs less than three cents a box to manufacture.

*Directions for Use.*—Use a damp woolen rag, dip in the box, and apply to the stove. Then polish with a dry cloth, and a most beautiful polish will appear.

TO FROST WINDOW PANES.—Take Epsom Salts and dissolve in beer. Apply with a brush and you have the finest window frosting known.

THE HOUSEKEEPER'S FRIEND, or ELECTRIC POWDER.—This is one of the most salable articles of the day and staple as flour—something that every housekeeper will buy. It is used for gold and silver plated ware, German silver, brass, copper, glass, tin, steel, or any material where a brilliant lustre is required. Is put up in two ounce wood boxes, costs three cents to manufacture, sells at retail for 25 cents, to agents and stores for $12.00 per 100 boxes.

RECIPE.—To four pounds best quality Whiting, add one-half pound Cream Tartar and three ounces Calcined Magnesia; mix thoroughly together, box and label.

*Directions.*—Use the polish dry with a piece of chamois skin or Canton flannel, previously moistened with water or alcohol, and finish with the polish dry. A few moments' rubbing will develop a surprising lustre, different from the polish produced by any other substance.

RECIPE.—Follow the same directions as in "Starch Enamel," and perfume as follows: Take two ounces Oil Lemon Grass and one-half ounce Oil of Cloves, and one-fourth ounce Oil of Lavender flowers; mix them well together. For this amount of perfume you require about four quarts of the liquid paraffine. Pour the oils into the melted paraffine while warm, stirring it well while pouring. Stamp into square cakes and put into neatly printed envelopes. Sell for ten cents a cake, cost two cents. Agents can sell 100 cakes a day.

THE LIGHTNING INK ERASER.—The great Lightning Ink Eraser may be used instead of a knife or scraper for erasing in order to rectify a mistake or clean off a blot, without injury to the paper, leaving the paper as clean and good to write upon as it was before the blot or mistake was made, and without injury to the printer's ink upon any printed form or ruling upon any first-class paper. Take of Chloride of Lime one pound, thoroughly pulverized, and four quarts of Soft Water. The above must be thoroughly shaken when first put together. It is required to stand twenty-four hours to dissolve the Chloride of Lime. Then strain through a cotton cloth, after which add a teaspoonful of Acetic Acid (No. 8 commercial) to every ounce of Chloride of Lime Water. The eraser is used by reversing the penholder in the hand, dipping the end in the fluid, and applying it, without rubbing, to the blot to be erased. When the ink has disappeared, absorb the fluid into a blotter, and the paper is immediately ready to write upon. Put up in common ink bottles and retail for 25 cents each.

THE MAGIC ANNIHILATOR.—To make one gross eight-ounce bottles—aqua ammonia one gallon, soft water eight gallons, best white soap four pounds, saltpetre eight ounces. Shave the soap fine, add the water, boil until the soap is dissolved, let it get cold, then add the saltpetre, stirring until dissolved. Now strain, let the suds settle, skim off the dry suds, add the ammonia, bottle and cork at once. Cost about $7.25 per gross; sells for $72.00. It will do everything claimed for it and more, too. It is no mixture of soap suds as some may suppose, but a pure scientific, chemical preparation. If you wish to make a small quantity for trial, take aqua ammonia two ounces, soft water one quart, saltpetre one teaspoonful. Shave the soap fine, mix all, shake well, and let settle a day or two to dissolve the soap.

*What It Will Do.*—It will remove all kinds of grease and oil spots from every variety of wearing apparel, such as coats, pants, vests, dress goods, carpets, etc., without injury to the finest silks or laces. It will shampoo like a charm, raising the lather in proportion to the amount of dandruff and grease in the hair. A cloth wet with it will remove all grease from door-knobs, window sills, etc., handled by kitchen domestics in their daily routine of kitchen work. It will remove paint from a board, I care not how hard or dry it is, if oil is used in the paint, yet it will not injure the finest textures. Its chemical action is such that it turns any oil or grease into soap, which is easily washed out with clear cold water. For cleaning silver, brass and copper ware it can't be beat. It is certain death to bed bugs, for they will never stop after they have encountered the Magic Annihilator.

*Directions for Use.*—For grease spots, pour upon the article to be cleaned a sufficient quantity of the Magic Annihilator rubbing well with a clean sponge, and applying to both sides of the article you are cleaning. Upon carpets and coarse goods, where the grease is hard and dry, use a stiff brush and wash out with clear cold water. Apply again if necessary. One application is all that is needed for any fresh grease spots, but for old or dried a second may be required. For shampooing take a small quantity of the Magic Annihilator with an equal quantity of water, apply to the hair with a stiff brush, brushing into the pores of the scalp, and wash out with clear water. You will be surprised at the silk gloss of your hair. For cleaning silver ware, etc., buy five cents' worth of whitening, mix a small quantity with the magic annihilator, and apply with a rag, rubbing briskly. For killing bed bugs, apply to the places they frequent, and they will leave in short order. You will find it useful in many other ways. (See price list of labels.)

# CHAPTER IX.

## MISCELLANEOUS DEPARTMENT.

FIRE-PROOF PAINT.—Take a sufficient quantity of Water for use; add as much Potash as can be dissolved therein. When the water will dissolve no more Potash, stir into the solution first, a quantity of flour paste of consistency of painter's size; second a sufficiency of pure clay to render it of the consistency of cream. Apply with a painter's brush.

N.B.—The above will admit of any coloring you please.

WATER-PROOF AND FIRE-PROOF CEMENT FOR ROOFS OF HOUSES.—Slack Stone Lime in a large tub or barrel with boiling water, covering the tub or barrel to keep in the steam. When thus slacked pass six quarts through a fine sieve. It will then be in a state of fine flour. To this add one quart Rock Salt and one gallon of Water. Boil the mixture and skim it clean. To every five gallons of this skimmed mixture add one pound of Alum and one-half pound Copperas; by slow degrees add three-fourths pound Potash and four quarts fine Sand or Wood Ashes sifted. Both of the above will admit of any coloring you please. It looks better than paint and is as durable as slate.

PAINT FOR ROUGH WOODWORK.—Six pounds melted Pitch, one pound Linseed Oil, and one pound Yellow Ochre.

SUPERIOR PAINT FOR BRICK HOUSES—To Lime Whitewash add, for a fastener, Sulphate of Zinc, and shade with any color you choose, as Yellow Ochre, Venetian Red, etc. It outlasts oil paint.

ART OF ETCHING ON COPPER.—Having obtained a piece of fine Copper, which will be well polished, make a mixture of Beeswax and a small quantity of Resin; melt these together, and when thoroughly incorporated by stirring, take a camel's hair brush and cover the plate, which must previously be warmed by the fire, with an even coating of the mixture.

When the mixture becomes hardened upon the plate, sketch the desired object upon the surface, then take an etching point, a large needle fixed in a handle will do, and cut through the wax to the surface of the copper, taking care to make the lines as distinct as possible.

This being done, raise a border of wax all around the plate, then pour strong Nitric Acid on the plate to the depth of an inch. The Acid will eat away the copper in those places which have been bared by the etching point. From time to time pour off the acid and wash the plate to see how the work is going on. Stop up with wax those places that appear to be etched deep enough, pour Acid upon the others, and let it remain until the process is completed. This done, melt off the wax clean the plate, and the etching is ready for the press. This is an employment from which a good remuneration may be derived.

MAHOGANY FURNITURE VARNISH.—Take of Proof Alcohol one quart, cut therein all the Gum Shellac it will take, add two ounces of Venice Turpentine, and coloring to suit. This makes a beautiful polish and will wear for years.

WATER-PROOF FOR LEATHER.—Take Linseed Oil one pint, Yellow Wax and White Turpentine each two ounces, Burgundy Pitch two ounces, melt and color with Lamp Black.

TO TAKE STAINS OUT OF MAHOGANY.—Mix Spirits of Salts six parts, Salt of Lemons one part, then drop a little on the stains, and rub them till they disappear.

CEMENTS.—Cements of various kinds should be kept for occasional use. Flour paste answers very well for slight purposes; if required stronger than usual, boil a little Glue or put some powdered Resin in it. White of Egg, or a solution of Glue and a strong Gum Water are good cements. A paste made of Linseed Meal dries very hard and adheres firmly. A soft cement is made of Yellow Wax, melted with its weight of Turpentine, and a little Venetian Red to give it color. This when cool is as hard as soap, and is very useful to stop up cracks, and is better to cover the corks of bottles than sealing wax or hard cement.

The best cement for broken china or glass is that sold under the name of Diamond cement; it is colorless and resists moisture. This is made by soaking Isinglass in water until it is soft, and then dissolving it in Proof Spirits; add to this a little Gum Ammoniac or Galbonam or Mastic, both dissolved in as little Alcohol as possible. When the cement is to be used, it must be gently liquified by placing the vial containing it in boiling water. The vial must be well closed with a good cork, not glass stopper, as they become forced. It is applied to the broken edges by a camel's hair pencil.

When objects are not to be exposed to the moisture, the White of an Egg alone is mixed with finely powdered Quicklime, will answer very well;

For patterns you can use any natural leaf, forming the creases in wax with thumb nail or needle. To put the flowers together, or the leaves on the stem, hold in the hand until warm enough to stick. If the sheeted wax is to be used in summer, put in a little Balsam of Fir to make it hard. If for winter, none will be required.

You can make many flowers without a teacher, but one to assist in the commencement would be a great help, though the most particular thing about it is to get the wax sheeted. The materials I have suggested can be procured at any drug store, and will cost from $3.00 to $4.50.

PORTABLE LEMONADE.—Tartaric Acid one ounce, White Sugar two pounds, Essense of Lemon one-fourth ounce; powder and keep dry for use. One dessert spoonful will make a glass of lemonade.

TO NEUTRALIZE WHISKY TO MAKE VARIOUS LIQUORS.—To forty gallons of Whisky add one and one-half pounds unslacked Lime, three-fourths of a pound of Alum, and one-half pint Spirits of Nitre. Stand twenty-four hours and draw it off.

MADEIRA WINE.—To four gallons prepared Cider, add one-fourth pound Tartaric Acid, four gallons of Spirits, three pounds Loaf Sugar. Let stand ten days, draw it off carefully. Fine it down, and again rack it in another cask.

SHERRY WINE.—To forty gallons prepared Cider add two gallons Spirits, three pounds of Raisins, six gallons good Sherry and one-half ounce Oil of Bitter Almonds, dissolved in Alcohol. Let it stand ten days, draw it off carefully. Fine it down, and again rack it in another cask.

ARTIFICIAL HONEY.—Take eight pounds of White Sugar, add two quarts of Water, boil four minutes, then add one pound of Bee's Honey. Strain while hot. Flavor with a drop of Oil of Peppermint and a drop of the Oil of Rose.

PORT WINE.—To forty gallons prepared Cider add six gallons good Port Wine, ten quarts Wild Grapes, clusters, one-half pound bruised Rhatany

Root, three ounces Tincture of Kino, three pounds Loaf Sugar, two gallons Spirits. Let this stand ten days. Color, if too light with Tincture of Rhatany, then rack it off and fine it. This should be repeated until the color is perfect and the liquid clear.

CLEANING COMPOUND.—Mix one ounce of Borax and one ounce Gum Camphor with one quart of boiling water. When cool add one pint of Alcohol, bottle and cork tightly. When wanted for use, shake well and sponge the garments to be cleaned. This is an excellent mixture for cleaning soiled black cashmere and woolen dresses, coat collars and black felt hats.

SHAVING SOAP.—Good white Soap in fine shavings, three pounds; Balm Soap, one pound; Soft Water, three-fourths of a pound; Soda, one ounce. Melt carefully over a slow fire in an earthen vessel; then add Oil of Lavender sixty drops, Oil of Lemon forty drops; mix well and make into forms.

LEATHER CEMENT.—Take Gutta Percha cut in Chloroform to right consistency for use. Equal to Cook's best for putting patches on leather, cloth shoes or boots. Well worth $100.

TO FASTEN PAPER TO TIN.—Take good clear pale yellow Glue, break it into rather small pieces, and let it soak a few hours in cold water. Pour off the supernatant water, place the glue thus softened in a wide-mouthed bottle; add sufficient Glacial Acid to cover the Glue, and facilitate the solution by standing the bottle in warm water. This Acetic will stick almost anything.

HUNTERS' AND TRAPPER'S SECRET.—Take equal parts of Oil of Rhodium, Anise Oil, Sweet Oil and Honey, and mix well. Put a few drops on any kind of bait. For musk-rats use sweet apples or vegetables for bait. For mink use a chicken's head or a piece of fresh meat.

FIRE KINDLERS—To make very nice fire kindlers take Resin, any quantity, and melt it, putting in for each pound being used two or three ounces or Tallow, and when all is hot stir in Pine Sawdust to make very thick, and while very hot spread it out about one inch thick, upon boards which have fine Sawdust sprinkled upon them to prevent it from sticking. When cold break up into lumps about an inch square. But if for sale take a thin board and press upon it while yet warm, to lay it off into inch squares. This makes it break regularly, if you press the crease sufficiently deep. Grease the marked board to prevent it sticking.

RED SEALING WAX.—Purchase four pounds Shellac, one and one-half pounds Veneer Turpentine, three pounds finest Cinnabar, and four ounces Venetian; mix the whole well together and melt over a very slow fire. Pour it on a thick, smooth glass, or any other flat smooth surface, and make it into three, six or ten sticks.

FURNITURE POLISH.—Equal parts Sweet Oil and Vinegar and a pint of Gum Arabic finely powdered. Shake the bottle and apply with a rag. It will make furniture look as good as new.

BLACK SEALING WAX.—Purchase the best Black Resin three pounds, Beeswax one-half pound, and finely powdered Ivory Black one pound. Melt the whole together over a slow fire, and make it into sticks.

CEMENT FOR LEATHER.—Virgin India Rubber dissolved in Bisulphide of Carbon. Add Bisulphide until of proper consistency to apply. After applying hold a moderately warm iron over the patch.

AROMATIC SCHIEDAM SCHNAPPS, to imitate.—To twenty-five gallons good common Gin, five over proof, add fifteen pints strained Honey, two gallons clear Water, five pints White Sugar Syrup, five pints Spirits of Nutmeg, mixed with Nitric Ether, five pints Orange Flower Water, seven quarts pure Water, one ounce Acetic Ether, eight drops Oil of Wintergreen dissolved with the Acetic Ether. Mix all the ingredients well; if necessary, fine with Alum and Salt of Tartar.

CHAMPAGNE CIDER.—Good Cider, pale, one hogshead, Spirits three gallons, Honey or Sugar twenty pounds. Mix and let them stand for two weeks; then fine with skimmed Milk one-half gallon. This will be very pale, and a similar article, when bottled in champagne bottles and silvered and labeled, has often been sold to the ignorant for champagne.

CIDER WITHOUT APPLES.—To one gallon of cold Water add dark brown Sugar one pound, Tartaric Acid one-half ounce, Yeast three tablespoonfuls. Shake well together.

ST. CROIX RUM.—To forty gallons p. or n. Spirits add two gallons St. Croix Rum, two ounces Acetic Acid, one and one-half ounces Butyric Acid, three pounds Loaf Sugar.

IRISH OR SCOTCH WHISKY.—To forty gallons proof Spirits add sixty drops Creosote dissolved in one quart of Alcohol, two ounces Acetic Acid, one pound Loaf Sugar. Stand forty-eight hours.

FRENCH BRANDY.—Pure Spirits one gallon, best French Brandy for any kind you wish to imitate, one quart, Loaf Sugar two ounces, Sweet Spirits Nitre one-half ounce, a few drops of Tincture of Catechu or Oak Bark, to roughen the taste, if desired, and color to suit.

ENGLISH GIN.—Plain Malt Spirits one hundred gallons, Spirits of Turpentine one pint, Bay Salt seven pounds. Mix and distill. The difference in the flavor of Gin is produced by varying the proportion of Turpentine, and by occasionally adding a small quantity of Juniper Berries.

FRENCH FURNITURE POLISH.—Alcohol 98 per cent one pint, Gum Copal and Shellac of each one ounce, Dragon's Blood. Mix and dissolve by setting in a warm place.

TO TAKE FAC-SIMILES OF SIGNATURES.—Write your name on a piece of paper, and while the ink is wet sprinkle over it some finely powdered Gum Arabic, then make a rim around it and pour on it some Fusible Alloy in a liquid state. Impressions may be taken from the plates formed in this way by means of printing ink and a copperplate press.

CHEMICAL COMPOUND.—Aqua Ammonia two ounces, soft Water one quart, Saltpetre one teaspoonful, Shaving Soap in shavings one ounce. Mix all together. Dissolve the Soap well, and any grease or dirt that cannot be removed with this preparation nothing else need be tried for it.

DISTILLING WHISKY FROM MOLASSES.—Take five gallons of Molasses, mix thoroughly with twenty-five gallons soft Water in a barrel. Stir in one-half gallon Brewer's Yeast; let it set from five to seven days in a warm place, say 70 degrees. During this time fermentation will proceed, which is known by a bubbling sensation. When this subsides it is ready for distilling. To distill use a common washing boiler, with the top well closed and a hole in the same, or thimble soldered on for the steam to pass through a pipe. Connect a tin pipe, say two inches in diameter and ten feet long with a short elbow end to the boiler; let the other end incline downward. Fill the boiler one-half full of the fermented wort, boil slowly and regularly until there is no taste of spirits left. The atmosphere condenses the steam. In this case if it should not entirely condense it lengthen or enlarge the pipe. The liquid thus obtained is low wines, and to use the same process of running proof spirits can be obtained. To continue this daily any given amount of molasses, etc., can be mixed, say one barrel each day. Five quarts can be obtained from four quarts of common molasses.

Intoxicating liquors of any and all kinds are the father of crime, the mother of abomination, the devil's best friend, and God's worst enemy.

INK POWDER.—Powdered Nut Galls four ounces, Copperas three ounces, Logwood one ounce, Gum Arabic one-half ounce. Sufficient for one quart of water.

FLORIDA WATER.—Dissolve in one-half gallon of 90 per cent Alcohol, one ounce each of Oil of Lavender, Oil of Bergamot and Oil of Lemon and Oil of Cloves and Cinnamon, one drachm each; add one gallon of Water and filter.

MOLASSES CANDY.—Boil Molasses over a moderately hot fire, stirring constantly. When you think it is done drop a little on a plate, and if sufficiently boiled it will be hard. Add a small quantity of Vinegar to render it brittle and any flavoring ingredient you prefer. Pour in buttered tin pans. If nuts are to be added strew them in the pans before pouring out the candy.

TO MAKE EGGS OF PHARAOH'S SERPENTS.—Take Mercury and dissolve it in moderately diluted Nitric Acid by means of heat, take care, however, that there be always an excess of Metallic Mercury remaining. Decant the solution and pour it in a solution of Sulphocyanide of Ammonia or Potassium, which may be bought at a good drug store or of a dealer in chemicals. Equal weights of both will answer. A precipitate will fall to the bottom of the beaker or jar, which is to be collected on a filter, and washed two or three times with water, when it is put in a warm place to dry. Take for every pound of this material one ounce of Gum Tragacanth, which has been soaked in hot water. When the gum is completely softened, it is to be transferred to a mortar, and then pulverized and dried precipitate gradually mixed with it, by means of a little water, so as to present a somewhat dried pill mass, from which, by hand, pellets of the desired size are formed, put on a piece of glass, and dried again. They are then ready for use.

BOOT AND SHOE BLACKING.—Ivory Black one pound, Molasses two ounces, Olive Oil four ounces, Oil of Vitriol four ounces, Alcohol eight ounces, Rye Flour one pound. Mix them together in a kettle.

ANGLER'S SECRET NO. 1.—Mix the juice of Lovage or Smellage, or spoiled cheese, with any kind of bait.

No. 2.—Mullen Seed pulverized and mixed with dough, and sprinkled on the surface of still water, intoxicates fish and makes them turn up on the top of the water.

BRISTOL'S TOOTH POWDER.—Prepared Chalk one pound, Castile Soap one-half pound, powdered Yellow Bark two ounces, powdered Gum Myrrh two ounces, powdered Loaf Sugar two ounces, powdered Orris two ounces; mix intimately, after having first pulverized the Castile Soap.

ROYAL WASHING POWDER.—Mix any quantity of Soda Ash with an equal portion of Carbonate of Soda—ordinary Soda—crushed into coarse grains. Have a thin solution of Glue, or decoction of Linseed Oil ready, into which pour the Soda until quite thick. Spread it out on boards in a warm apartment to dry. As soon as dry, shake up well, so that it will pack easily into nice square packages. Label neatly. Pound packages cost seven cents; retails for thirty-five cents.

EGYPTIAN CEMENT.—For mending china, glass or woodenware: Take one pound of the best White Glue, one-half pound dry White Lead, one quart soft Water, one-half pint Alcohol. Put the three first articles in a dish, and that dish in a pot of boiling water. Let it boil until dissolved, then add the Alcohol, and boil again until mixed. A little Camphor should be added, to preserve it and disguise its composition. Put in small bottles; 25 cents each.

"HANDY" WATER PENS.—Take best quality violet Analine, reduce to a thick paste with water; then add Mucilage and mix thoroughly. Apply the paste thus made to the pen, and let it dry twelve hours Any steel pen may be prepared in this way. We always keep in stock the best violet Analine, also a large stock of pens.

*Directions for Using.*—Start action by dipping into water up to filling. If pen should be greasy, wet point with the tongue. To make the ink flow thick, dip to the filling; if wanted thin or pale, dip only to the eye of the pen after starting. After using throw the water off, but don't wipe it, for it will dry in a minute.

ARTIFICIAL OYSTERS.—Grate green corn in a dish; to one pint of this add one egg well beaten, small teacup of flour, half a cup of butter, salt and pepper; mix well together and fry them brown.

PASTE THAT WILL NOT SOUR.—Dissolve one-half of an ounce of Alum in a pint of boiling water, add an equal weight of Flour, made smooth in a little cold water, and a few drops of Oil of Cloves, and let the whole come to a boil. Put it into glass or ointment jars. It will keep for months.

ESSENCES are made with one ounce of any given oil added to one pint of Alcohol. Peppermint is colored with Tincture Turmeric, Cinnamon with Tincture Red Saunders, Wintergreen with Tincture Kino.

TINCTURES are made with one ounce of Gum, Root, or Bark, etc., dried, to each pint of proof spirits and let it stand one week and filter.

OLEOMARGARINE MANUFACTURE.—The process by which suet is converted into the substance called oleamargarine is as follows: The crude suet after first being washed in cold water is "rendered," melted, and then drawn off into movable tanks. The hard substance is subjected to a hydraulic pressure of 350 tons, and the oil extracted. The butter is made from the oil thus obtained, while the hard substance remaining is disposed of as stearine. The oil, being carried off into churns, is mixed with milk and from three to five per cent of dairy butter. It is then drawn off in a consistent form, and cooled with broken ice. The latter is soon removed, and the butter worked up with a small portion of salt. When this is done the article is ready for packing and consumption.

SILVER PLATING FLUID.—Take one ounce Precipitate Silver to one-half ounce Cyanite of Potash and one-fourth ounce of Hyposulphate of Soda. Put all in a quart of water, add a little Whiting, and shake before using. Apply with a soft rag. Put up in ounce bottles, and retail for 25 cents. The secret is worth $100 to an agent to sell to families.

MUCILAGE FOR LABELS.—Dextrine two ounces, Glycerine one drachm, Alcohol one ounce, water six ounces.

FIG CANDY.—Take one pound of Sugar and one pint of Water, set over a slow fire. When done add a few drops of Vinegar and a lump of Butter, and pour into a pan in which Figs are laid.

RAISIN CANDY.—Can be made in the same manner, substituting stoned raisins for the Figs. Common Molasses Candy is very nice with any kind of nuts added.

PEPPERMINT, ROSE, or HOARHOUND CANDY.—These may be made as Lemon Candy. Flavor with Essence of Rose, or Peppermint, or finely powdered Hoarhound. Pour it out in a buttered paper, placed in a square tin pan.

COLOGNE.—Take one gallon 95 per cent Alcohol or Cologne Spirits, two ounces Oil of Bergamot, one-half ounce Orange, one-half ounce Oil of Cedar, one-half drachm Oil of Nevio, one-half drachm Oil Rosemary. Mix well and it is fit for use. A nice article.

BAY RUM, EQUAL TO THE BEST IMPORTED.—Oil of Bay, fine, one and one-half drachms, Oil of Neroli (bigard) ten drops, Ether Acetic two drachms, Alcohol deod. (strong) three pints, Water, two and one-fourth pints, Caromel sufficient to tinge. Let it stand two weeks and filter.

COPYING PAD.—White Gelatine four ounces, Water eight ounces, Glycerine eight ounces, Gum Dextrine two ounces. Always use these same proportions for any amount. Melt the Gelatine in the water at a gentle heat, add to it the Glycerine, in which the Gum Dextrine has been thoroughly incorporated. Now stir all together until thoroughly mixed and then pour into pans of the desired size, to the depth of one-half inch.

*Recipe for Ink to Be Used.*—Violet Analine forty grains, Gum Arabic twelve grains, Alcohol one-fourth ounce, Water one-half ounce. Dissolve the Gum in the Water and Alcohol, then add the Analine. Shake in a bottle from time to time until the Analine is dissolved.

*To work the Copying Pad.*—Write with ink on any good paper, press the written surface on the pad and allow it to remain two minutes; then take off and the writing will remain, from which impressions may be taken by laying on plain paper, and smoothing with the hand. As soon as the last impression is taken be sure and wash off with a wet sponge.

TO BORE HOLES IN GLASS.—Any hard steel tool will cut glass with great facility when kept freely wet with camphor dissolved in turpentine. A drill bow may be used, or even the hand alone. A hole bored may be readily enlarged by a round file. The ragged edges of glass vessels may also be thus easily smoothed by a flat file. Flat window glass can be readily sawed by a watch spring saw by aid of this solution. In short the most brittle glass can be wrought almost as easily as brass by the use of cutting tools kept constantly moist with Camphorized Oil of Turpentine.

TO ETCH UPON GLASS.—Procure several thick, clear pieces of crown glass; and immerse them in Melted Wax, so that they may receive a complete coating, or pour over them a solution of Wax in Benzine. When perfectly cold draw on them with a fine steel point, flowers, trees, houses, portraits, etc. Whatever parts of the drawings are intended to be corroded with the acid should be perfectly free from the least particle of wax. When all these drawings are finished the pieces of glass must be immersed one by one in a square leaden box or receiver, where they are to be submitted to the action of Hydroflouric Acid Gas, made by acting on Powdered Flour-Spar by Concentrated Sulphuric Acid. When the glasses are sufficiently corroded, they are to be taken out, and the wax is to be removed by first dipping them in warm and then in hot water, or by washing with turpentine or benzine. Various colors may be applied to the corroded parts of the glass, whereby a fine painting may be executed. In the same manner sentences and initials of names may be etched on wine-glasses, tumblers, etc.

RUBBER HAND STAMPS.—Set up the desired name and address in common type, oil the type, and place a guard about one-half inch high around the form. Now mix Plaster of Paris to the desired consistency, pour in and allow it to set. Have your Vulcanized Rubber all ready, as made in long strips three inches wide and one-eighth of an inch thick, cut off the size of the intended stamp. Remove the plaster cast from the type, and place both the cast and the rubber in a screw press, applying sufficient heat to thoroughly soften the rubber, then turn down the screw hard, and let it remain until the rubber receives the exact impression of the cast and becomes cold, when it is removed, neatly trimmed with a sharp knife, and cemented to the handle, ready for use.

COMMON TWIST CANDY.—Boil three pounds of common Sugar and one pint of water over a slow fire for half an hour without skimming. When boiled enough take it off, rub your hands over with butter; take that which is a little cooled and pull it as you would molasses candy, until it is white; then twist or braid it and cut it up in strips.

STICKY FLY PAPER.—Boiled Linseed Oil and Rosin; melt and add honey. Soak the paper in a strong solution of Alum, then dry before applying the above.

KISS-ME-QUICK.—Spirits one gallon, Essence of Thyme one-fourth ounce, Essence of Orange Flowers two ounces, Essence of Neroli one-half ounce, Otto of Roses thirty drops, Essence of Jasmine one ounce, Essence of Balm Mint one-half ounce, Petals of Roses four ounces, Oil of Lemon twenty drops, Calorous Aromaticus one-half ounce, Essence Neroli one-fourth ounce. Mix and strain.

HOW TO TEST THE RICHNESS OF MILK.—Procure any long glass vessel—a cologne bottle or long phial. Take a narrow strip of paper, just the length from the neck to the bottom of the phial, and mark it off with 100 lines at equal distances, or into fifty lines, and count each as two, and paste upon the phial so as to divide its length into 100 equal parts. Fill it to the highest mark with milk fresh from the cow, and allow it to stand in a perpendicular position 24 hours. The number of spaces occupied by the cream will give you its exact percentage in the milk without any guess work.

FINE PEPPERMINT LOZENGES.—Best powdered White Sugar seven pounds, pure Starch one pound, Oil of Peppermint to flavor. Mix with Mucilage.

HOW TO FASTEN RUBBER TO WOOD AND METAL.—As rubber plates and rings are nowadays used almost exclusively for making connections between steam and other pipes and apparatus, much annoyance is often experienced by the impossibility or imperfection of an air-tight connection. This is obviated entirely by employing a cement which fastens alike well to the rubber and to the metal or wood. Such cement is prepared by a solution of Shellac in Ammonia. This is best made by soaking pulverized Gum Shellac in ten times its weight of strong Ammonia, when a slimy mass is obtained, which in three or four weeks will become liquid without the use of hot water. This softens the rubber and becomes, after volatilization of the Ammonia, hard and impermeable to gases and fluids.

TO TRANSFER PRINTED MATTER AND PRINT FROM IT AGAIN.—Take your picture or print and soak it for a short time in a weak solution of Caustic Potash, then remove it carefully, and let it dry on a sheet of clean paper. Then take a piece of copper, zinc, or steel, which has previously been well cleaned, and dip it into hot white wax. Let the first coat set, then dip again. Having got the plate thoroughly coated and set, lay the matter to be transferred on the plate, and rub it gently all over on the back; now raise it up, and it will be transferred on to the wax on the plate. Now take needles of a different thickness, and scrawl all over the wax, following the lines of the engraving. Having got the picture all traced out, pour upon it some weak acid if you use zinc, which is too soft to print many from, therefore it is better to use copper or steel. If you use copper, make the following solution to pour over it: Verdigris four parts, Salt four parts, Sal Ammoniac four parts, Alum one part, Water sixteen parts, Sour Vinegar twelve parts. Dissolve by heat. For steel, use Pyroligneous Acid five parts, Alcohol one part, Nitric Acid one part. Mix the first two, then add the Nitric Acid. Pouring the preparations over the plates where the traces of the pictures are, it will eat into the metal plate without affecting the wax. Let it stand till it has eaten a sufficient depth, then wash the plate with cold water, dry it and place it near the fire till all the wax is melted off. You can now print as many as you please from the plate by rubbing on it printer's ink, so as to fill all the fine spaces; which, when done, wipe it over smoothly with clean cloths to remove the superfluous ink which is on the face of the plate. Now take damp paper or cardboard, and press it on the plate, either with a copying press or the hand, and you get a fine impression, or as many as you want by repeating the inking process. I would recommend beginners to try their skill with valueless prints before attempting to make transfers of fine engravings, as the picture to be transferred is destroyed by the process.

I.X.L. BAKING POWDER.—Take one pound Tartaric Acid in Crystals, one and one-half pounds Bi-Carbonate of Soda, and one and one-half pounds of Potash Starch. Each must be powdered separately, well dried by a slow heat, well mixed through a sieve. Pack hard in tinfoil, tin or paper glazed on the outside. The Tartaric Acid and Bi-Carbonate of Soda can of course be bought cheaper of wholesale druggists than you can make them, unless you are doing things on a large scale, but Potato Starch any one can make. It is only necessary to peel the potatoes and to grate them up fine into vessels of water, to let them settle, pour off the water, and make the settlings into balls, and dry them. With these directions anyone can make as good baking-powder as is sold anywhere. If he wants to make it very cheap, he can take Cream of Tartar and common Washing (Carbonate) Soda, instead of the articles named in the recipe, but this would be advisable only where customers insist on excessively low prices in preference to quality of goods.

EVERLASTING FENCE POSTS.—I discovered many years ago that wood could be made to last longer than iron in the ground, but thought the process so simple and inexpensive that it was not worth while to make any stir about it. I would as soon have poplar, basswood, or quaking ash as any other kind of timber for fence posts. I have taken out basswood posts after having been set seven years, which were as sound when taken out as when they were first put in the ground. Time and weather seem to have no effect on them. The posts can be prepared for less than two cents apiece. This is the recipe: Take boiled Linseed Oil and stir it in pulverized Charcoal to the consistency of paint. Put a coat of this over the timber, and there is not a man that will live to see it rot.

LIQUID GLUE.—To one ounce of Borax in one pint of boiling water, add two ounces of Shellac, and boil until the Shellac is dissolved.

TO MEND TINWARE BY THE HEAT OF A CANDLE.—Take a phial about two-thirds full of Muriatic Acid and put into it little bits of Sheet Zinc as long as it dissolves them; then put in a crumb of Sal Ammoniac and fill up with water and it is ready to use. Then with the cork of the phial, wet the place to be mended with the preparation; then put a piece of Zinc over the hole and hold a lighted candle or spirit lamp under the place, which melts the solder on the tin, and causes the zinc to adhere without further trouble. Wet the zinc also with the solution; or a little solder may be put on instead of the zinc or with the zinc.

TO WHITEN AND SOFTEN THE HANDS.—Take one-half lb. Mutton Tallow, one ounce Camphor Gum, one ounce Glycerine; melt, and when thoroughly mixed, set away to cool. Rub the hands with this every night.

A BRANDING INK.—A waterproof branding ink, good for marking sheep: Shellac two ounces, Borax two ounces, Water twenty-four ounces, Gum Arabic two ounces, Lamp Black sufficient. Boil the Borax and Shellac in the water till they are dissolved, and withdraw them from the fire. When the solution becomes cold, complete 25 ounces with water, and add Lamp Black enough to bring the preparation to a suitable consistency. When it is to be used with a stencil it must be made thicker than when it is used with a brush. The above gives black ink. For red ink substitute Venetian Red for Lamp Black; for blue Ultramarine; and for green a mixture of Ultramarine and Chrome Yellow.

FRENCH POLISH, or DRESSING FOR LEATHER.—Mix two pints best Vinegar with one pint soft water. Stir into it one-fourth pound Glue, broken up, one-half pound Logwood chips, one-fourth ounce finely powdered Indigo, one-fourth ounce best soft Soap, and one-fourth Isinglass. Put the mixture over the fire, and let it boil ten minutes or more; then strain, bottle and cork. When cold it is fit for use. Apply with a sponge.

NEW YORK BARBER'S STAR HAIR OIL.—Castor Oil six and one-half pints, Alcohol one and one-half pints, Citronella and Lavender Oil, each one-half ounce.

BARBER'S SHAMPOOING MIXTURE.—Soft Water one pint, Sal Soda one ounce, Cream Tartar one-fourth ounce. Apply thoroughly to the hair.

CRUCIBLES.—The best crucibles are made of a pure fire clay, mixed with finely ground cement of oil crucibles, and a portion of black lead or graphite; some pounded coke may be mixed with the plumbago. The clay should be prepared in a similar way as for making pottery ware. The vessels, after being formed, must be slowly dried, and then properly baked in a kiln.

*Black Lead Crucibles* are made of two parts of Graphite and one of Fire Clay, mixed with Water into a paste, pressed in moulds, and well dried, but not baked hard in the kiln. This compound forms excellent small or portable furnaces.

## WHAT TO INVENT, AND HOW TO PROTECT YOUR INVENTION.

WHAT TO INVENT.—Cheap, useful articles that will sell at sight. Something that everyone needs, and the poorest can afford. Invent simple things for the benefit of the masses, and your fortune is made. Some years back a one-armed soldier amassed a fortune from a single toy—a wooden ball attached to a rubber string. They cost scarcely anything, yet millions were sold at a good price. A German became enormously rich by patenting a simple wooden plug for beer barrels. "What man has done, man may do."

HOW TO PROTECT YOUR INVENTION.—Patent it. If you do not, others will reap the benefits that rightfully belong to you.

A PATENT IS A PROTECTION given to secure the inventor in the profits arising from the manufacture and sale of an article of his own creation.

TO WHOM LETTERS PATENT ARE GRANTED.—Section 4886 of the Revised Statutes of the United States provides that: "Any person who has invented or discovered any new and useful art, machine, manufacture or composition of matter, or any new and useful improvement thereof, not known or used by others in this country, and not patented or described in any printed publication in this or any foreign country, before his invention or discovery thereof, and not in public use, or on sale for more than two years prior to his application, unless the same is proved to have been abandoned, may, upon the payment of the fees required by law, and other due proceedings had, obtain a patent therefor."

And section 4888 of the same Statute enacts:

Section 4888. Before any inventor or discoverer shall receive a patent for his invention or discovery, he shall make application therefor, in writing, to the Commissioner of Patents, and shall file in the Patent Office a written description of the same, and of the manner and process of making, constructing, compounding, and using it, in such full, clear, concise and exact terms, as to enable any person skilled in the art or science to which it appertains, or with which it is most nearly connected, to make, construct, compound, and use the same; and in case of a machine, he shall explain the principle thereof and the best mode in which he has contemplated applying that principle, so as to distinguish it from other inventions; and he shall particularly point out and distinctly claim that part, improvement or combination which he claims as his invention or discovery. The specification and claim shall be signed by the inventor and attested by two witnesses.

It is also required by law that when "The case admits of drawings," it shall be properly illustrated; and also, if the Commissioner requires it, that a model shall be furnished in cases capable of such demonstration.

The cost of obtaining Letters Patent in ordinary cases is: First, Government fees, $15; counsel fees, including drawings, $25; second, or final Government fees, to be paid within six months from date of allowance, $20; total, $60.

DESIGNS.—A design patent can be obtained for novelties in the shape of configuration of articles, or impressions by any means whatever. These patents are of great value to the trade.

The Government fees for a design patent are:

    On filing every application for a design patent     $10.00

    On issuing a design patent for 3½ years no further charge.

    On issuing a design patent for 7 years     5.00

    On issuing a design patent for 14 years     20.00

CAVEATS.—A caveat is a confidential communication used in the Patent Office, and it consists of a specification, drawings, oath and petition. The specification must contain a clear description of the intended invention.

HOW A COPYRIGHT IS SECURED.—The method by which a copyright is obtained under the revised acts of Congress is as simple and inexpensive as can be reasonably asked. All unnecessary red tape is dispensed with, and the cost to the author who is seeking thus to protect himself in the enjoyment of the profits of his work, is so small as to be scarcely appreciable. This is an example of cheapness and directness toward which all branches of public administration should tend, if a government is to fulfill its proper mission of serving the people without needlessly taxing them. Directions have lately been issued for the guidance of persons wishing to obtain copyrights; and, as many of our readers may not be conversant with the subject, we give a brief abstract of the process.

The first thing necessary is to send a printed copy of the title of the work, plainly directed to "Librarian of Congress, Washington, D.C." The copyright law applies not only to books, pamphlets and newspapers, but also to maps, charts, photographs, paintings, drawings, music, statuary, etc. If there is a title page, send that; if not, a title must be printed expressly for the purpose, and in both cases the name of the author or claimant of copyright must accompany the title. Use no smaller paper than commercial note.

A remittance of one dollar must be made along with the application. This is the whole charge—half of it being for the entry on the record, and the other half for your certificate, which the Librarian will send you promptly by mail. You will of course prepay your postage.

Within ten days after your book, or other article, is published, you are required to send two complete copies of the best edition to the Librarian, addressed as before, prepaying postage; or the Librarian will furnish "penalty labels," under which they can be sent free of postage. If this deposit of copies is neglected, the copyright is void, and you are liable to fine of $25.

The law requires that on the title page of a copyrighted work, or some part of the drawing, painting, statue, or whatever it may be, there shall be printed these words: "Entered according to act of Congress, in the year ——, by ——, in the office of the Librarian of Congress, at Washington;" or, if preferred, this briefer form may be used: "Copyright, 18—, by ——." To this may be added, "Right of translation reserved," or "All rights reserved;" but in that case the Librarian must have been duly notified, so that he may include it in the record.

Any person who prints the copyright notice on his work without having obtained a copyright, is liable to a penalty of $1.00. The original term of a copyright runs for twenty-eight years, and it may then be renewed for a further term of fourteen years, either by the author or by his widow or children, application being made not less than six months before the expiration of the right. Trade marks and labels cannot be copyrighted under this law, but are provided for by a separate act, relating to matters of detail, which cannot here be recited, but in regard to which, the Librarian at Washington will give the needed information whenever required.

TRADE MARKS, LABELS, PRINTS, ETC.—Copyrights cannot be granted upon trade marks, nor upon mere names of companies or articles, nor upon prints or labels intended to be used with any article of manufacture. If protection for such names or labels is desired, application must be made to the Patent Office, where they are registered at a fee of $6 for labels, and $25 for trade marks.

By the word "print" is meant any device, word, or figures (not a trade mark) impressed directly upon the article, to denote the name of the manufacturer, etc.

By the word "label" is meant a slip of paper, or other material, to be attached to manufactured articles, or to packages containing them, and bearing the name of the manufacturer, directions for use, etc.

WATER ICES.—Some make these with acid, water, flavor, and the whites of eggs. *No good.*

The best rules for the amount of sugar is to suit your taste.

FRANGIPANNA.—Spirits one gallon, Oil Bergamot one ounce, Oil of Lemon one ounce; macerate for four days, frequently shaking; then add Water one gallon, Orange Flower Water one pint, Essence of Vanilla two ounces. Mix.

SILVERING POWDER.—Nitrate of Silver and common Salt, of each thirty grains, Cream of Tartar three and one-half drachms. Pulverize finely, mix thoroughly, and bottle for use. Unequaled for polishing copper and plated goods.

EXTRACT OF LEMON.—Three ounces Oil Lemon; cut with 95 proof Alcohol; add one gallon 80 proof Alcohol, and filter through cotton or felt. Put up in two ounce bottles. Sells for 25 cents; jobs at $1.00 and $1.50 according to quality and style of package.

BALM OF A THOUSAND FLOWERS.—Deodorized Alcohol one pint, nice white Bar Soap four ounces; shave the soap when put in, stand in a warm place till dissolved, then add Oil of Citronella one drachm, and Oils of Neroli and Rosemary, of each one-half drachm.

TIN CANS.—Size of sheet for from 1 to 100 gallons:

| | | | |
|---|---|---|---|
| For 1 gallon | 7 by 20 ins. | For 25 gallons | 30 by 56 ins. |

| | | | |
|---|---|---|---|
| For 3½ gallons | 10 by 28 ins. | For 40 gallons | 36 by 63 ins. |
| For 5 gallons | 12 by 40 ins. | For 50 gallons | 40 by 70 ins. |
| For 6 gallons | 14 by 40 ins. | For 75 gallons | 40 by 84 ins. |
| For 10 gallons | 20 by 42 ins. | For 100 gallons | 40 by 98 ins. |
| For 15 gallons | 30 to 42 ins. | | |

This includes all laps, seams, etc., which will be found sufficiently correct for all practical purposes.

MOULDS AND DIES.—Copper, Zinc and Silver in equal proportions, melt together under a coat of powdered charcoal, and mould into the form you desire. Bring them to nearly a white heat, and lay on the thing you would take an impression of, press with sufficient force, and you will get a perfect and beautiful impression.

INDESTRUCTIBLE LAMP WICKS.—Steep common wicks in a concentrated aqueous solution of Tungstate of Soda, and then dry thoroughly in an oven.

A GOLD PLATE FOR SMALL ARTICLES, WITHOUT A BATTERY.—Digest a small fragment of gold with about ten times its weight of mercury until it is dissolved, shake the amalgam together in a bottle, and after cleansing the articles, coat them uniformly with the amalgam. Then expose them on an iron tray heated to low redness for a few minutes. The mercury volatilizes, leaving the gold attached as a thin coating to the article. The heating should be done in a stove, so that the poisonous mercurial fumes may pass up the chimney.

A GELATINE MOULD FOR CASTING PLASTER ORNAMENTS.—Allow twelve ounces of Gelatine to soak for a few hours in water, until it has absorbed as much as it can, then apply heat, by which it will liquify. If the mould is required to be elastic, add three ounces of Treacle, and mix well with the Gelatine. If a little Chrome Alum (precise proportions are immaterial) be added to the Gelatine, it causes it to lose its property of being again dissolved in water. A saturated solution of Bichromate of Potash brushed over the surface of the mould, allowed to become dry and afterwards exposed to sunlight for a few minutes, renders the surface so hard as to be unaffected by moisture.

IMITATION OF GROUND GLASS.—The following is from an Antwerp scientific journal. Paint the glass with the following varnishes: Sandarac eighteen drachms, Mastic four drachms, Ether twenty-four ounces, Benzine six to eighteen ounces. The more Benzine the coarser the grain of imitation glass will be.

UNSHRINKABLE PATTERNS.—The best mixture for small patterns, that does not shrink in casting, is sixty-nine parts Lead, fifteen and one-half parts Antimony, fifteen and one-half parts Bismuth, by weight. A cheap kind for finished patterns can be made of ten parts Zinc, one part Antimony, one part Tin.

TO MAKE ARTIFICIAL MARBLE FOR PAPER WEIGHTS OR OTHER FANCY ARTICLES.—Soak Plaster of Paris in a solution of Alum, bake it in an over, and then grind it to a powder. In using mix it with water, and to produce the clouds and veins stir in any dry color you wish; this will become very hard, and is susceptible of a very high polish.

MOLDS OF GLUE AND MOLASSES, SUCH AS RODGERS USES FOR MAKING HIS STATUETTES.—The flexible moulds referred to are prepared as follows: Glue eight pounds, Molasses (New Orleans) seven pounds. Soak the Glue over night in a small quantity of cold water, then melt it by heat over a salt water bath, stir until froth begins to rise, then add and stir in briskly the Molasses previously heated. Continue to heat and stir the mixture for about half an hour; then pour.

TO CLARIFY LIQUIDS.—The following composition is said to bleach all colored liquids, and to render bone-black perfectly unnecessary: Albumen three hundred, Neutral Tartrate of Potash two, Alum five, Sal Ammoniac seven hundred parts. The Albumen must of course not be coagulated. The ingredients are first dissolved in a little water and then added to the liquid to be clarified.

TO PREVENT STORE WINDOWS FROM STEAMING.—J. F. writes: I am about to have the front show windows of my store inclosed with inside windows. Can you tell any way to prevent the outside windows frosting in cold weather? A. Clean the glass occasionally with a cloth moistened with pure Glycerine, wiping it so as to leave only a trace of the Glycerine adhering to the surface—this on the inside.

ARTIFICIAL INDIA RUBBER.—A cheap and useful substitute for Indian rubber is prepared by mixing a thick solution of Glue with Tungstate of Soda and Hydrochloric Acid. A compound of Tungstic Acid and Glue is precipitated, which at a temperature of 86 degrees to 104 degrees F. is sufficiently elastic to admit of being drawn out into very thin sheets. On cooling this mass becomes solid and brittle, but on being heated is again soft and plastic. This new compound can be used for many of the purposes to which rubber is adapted.

RUBBER STAMPS FOR PHOTOGRAPHS.—Many photographers employ a rubber stamp for imprinting the backs of mounts, and in these circumstances a good ink is very essential. Here is the recipe for making one quoted from the *Engineer,* and said to yield an excellent ink which, while not drying on the pad, will yet not readily smear when impressed upon paper: Aniline Red (Violet) one hundred and eighty grains, distilled Water two ounces, Glycerine one teaspoonful, Treacle one-half teaspoonful. The crystals of Aniline are powdered and dissolved in the boiling distilled water, and the other ingredients then added.

A GOOD IDEA.—*How to Remove Pain and Soreness from Wounds.* The value of the smoke from burned wool to remove the pain and soreness from wounds of all kinds, or from sores, is great, and it will give immediately relief from the intense pain caused by a gathering. The easiest way to prepare this is to cut all-wool flannel—if you haven't the wool—into narrow strips, take some hot ashes with a few small live coals on a shovel, sprinkle some of the flannel strips on it, and hold the injured member in the smoke for five or ten minutes, using plenty of flannel to make a thick smoke. Repeat as often as seems necessary, though one smoking is usually enough.

CHILBLAINS.—We glean two prescriptions from the *British Medical Journal*. They are now being used in this country, and with good results. Lin. Belladonnæ two drachms, Lin. Aconita one drachm, Acid Carbolici six minims, Collod. Flexil one ounce.

Mix and apply every night with a camel's hair pencil, Collod. Flexil four drachms, Oleiricini four drachms, Spt. Tereb, four drachms. Use three times daily with camel's hair brush.

SAID TO BE GOOD FOR GRIP.—Anything that affords hope of relief from Grip is of interest. Pauline Crayson writes from Cranford, N.J., to *New York Tribune*, saying: "I have found Peroxide of Hydrogen (medicinal) a marvelous remedy in the treatment of grip and influenza. This medicine should be diluted with water and administered internally, and by snuffing through the nostrils or by spraying the nostrils and throat. I believe the good results from this treatment, which I have never known to fail of producing a speedy cure, are due to the destruction of the microbe upon which this disease depends." The remedy is simple and within the reach of everybody, and can easily be tested.

STICKS LIKE A BROTHER.—A paste that will adhere to anything.— Prof. Alex. Winchell is credited with the invention of a cement that will stick to anything (*Nat. Drug*). Take two ounces of clear Gum Arabic, one and one-half ounces of fine Starch and one-half ounce of White Sugar. Pulverize the Gum Arabic, and dissolve it in as much water as the laundress would use for the quality of starch indicated. Dissolve the starch and sugar in the gum solution. Then cook the mixture in a vessel suspended in boiling water until the starch becomes clear. The cement should be as thick as tar and keep so. It can be kept from spoiling by dropping in a lump of Gum Camphor, or a little Oil of Cloves or Sassafras. This cement is very strong indeed, and will stick perfectly to glazed surfaces, and is good to repair broken rocks, minerals or fossils. The addition of a small amount or Sulphate of Aluminum will increase the effectiveness of the paste, besides helping to prevent decomposition.

## DIRECTIONS FOR MAKING ALL KINDS OF CANDY.

MOLASSES TAFFY.—New Orleans Molasses one pint, Sugar one and one-half pounds, Water one-half pint (no doctor). Stir all the time to a good light snap. Lemon flavor. Work as above.

CREAM TAFFY.—Same as above. When to the ball degree have ready half cup cider vinegar, one-fourth pipe Cream Tartar, dissolve in the Vinegar, four ounces Butter. Add, stir, and work as you do the white taffy.

NUT TAFFY.—Use the cream taffy recipe. Just before the candy is done cooking stir in any kind of nut goodies, pour out, and when cool enough not to run, form it into a block, cut or break it with a hammer.

GOOD BROWN BUTTER-SCOTCH.—C Sugar, three pounds; Water, one and one-fourth pint; Cream Tartar, one full pipe dissolved in one cup Cider Vinegar; Molasses, one-half pint; Butter, eight ounces (no flavor). Add all except the Vinegar, Cream Tartar and Butter. Boil to medium ball, then add the Cream Tartar in the Vinegar and Butter. Stir all the time carefully. Boil to light snap finish as before in cheap Butter-Scotch.

SOUR LEMON DROPS.—Make a batch of barley squares. Just as soon as you pour it on the slab sprinkle over it three-fourths ounce dry Tartaric Acid, two tablespoons Lemon flavor; turn the cold edges in to the center of the batch, work it like bread dough; place this before a hot stove on your table and cut into little pieces with your scissors, or run the batch through a drop machine.

All goods that you want to spin out or run through a machine or cut with scissors should be kept warm by a sheet iron stove, on a brick foundation, fitted in the table evenly, and the candy placed in front to keep warm.

Should the candy slab, after it is greased, act sticky, not allowing the candy to come up freely, throw a dust of flour over the sticky place after it has been greased.

STICK CANDY.—Stick candy is made precisely the same as peppermint clips, by keeping the batch round, and a second person to twist them and keep them rolling until cold. This can be done only by practice. The sticks are then chopped in the desired length by heavy shears.

STRAWBERRY.—Same, only flavor with strawberry; color with liquid coloring slightly.

MAPLE CARAMELS.—Use one-half Maple Sugar with C Sugar. No flavor.

WALNUT CARAMELS.—Same as the first. When done, stir in sufficient nuts to suit.

A better caramel can be made with white sugar, and milk instead of water.

Still better, by using cream one quart, and when cream cannot be had, condensed milk dissolved in milk works fine.

ALMOND BARS.—Same as peanut, only add the Almond nuts in time to allow them to roast a little in the boiling sugar. One-fourth of a pint of New Orleans syrup added to the boiling sugar improves the flavor and color.

CHOCOLATE COATING.—Can use sweet confectioners', or confectioners' plain (never use the quarter and one-pound grocery packages, as it contains too much sugar to melt good). Place a small piece of paraffine the size of a hickory-nut and one small teaspoon of lard in a rice cooker, melt, add one-half pound of chocolate, stir until dissolved; dip balls of cream in this chocolate, drop on wax paper to cool, and you have fine hand made chocolate drops.

COLD SUGAR ICING.—For dipping cream drops. Confectioners' sugar with the white of eggs and a small amount of dissolved Gum Arabic in water. Make this into a batter. If thick, the drops will be rough; if thin, the drops will be smooth.

COCOANUT CREAM ICE.—Two pounds granulated sugar, three-fourths pint water, boil to a light crack; set off, add four ounces glucose (or the amount of cream tartar you can hold on the point of a penknife); set back on the fire, just let come to a boil to dissolve the glucose; set off again, add immediately one-fourth ounce shaved paraffine, six ounces cream dough cut up fine, one grated cocoanut. Stir all until it creams, pour out into a frame on brown paper dusted with flour, mark and cut with a knife when cold.

OPERA CREAMS.—Two pounds white sugar, three-fourths pint cow's cream, boil to a soft ball; set off; add two ounces glucose; set on, stir easy until it commences to boil, then pour out, let get three-fourths cold, and stir it until it turns into a cream. Then work into two tablespoons vanilla, line a pan with wax paper, flatten the batch in it, and mark it in squares. Set aside two hours to harden.

ITALIAN CREAM OPERAS.—Melt four ounces butter with four ounces plain chocolate. Take a batch of the opera cream; when cooked, add the above, stir it in the kettle until it creams, then pan and work it as you do the operas.

BUTTER CREAMS.—One and one-half pounds white sugar, and one-half pound C. sugar, three-fourths pound glucose, one-fourth pint molasses, one and one-fourth pint water; boil to the hard snap, add six ounces butter, set off until it melts; set on and let boil, to well mix the butter; pour out. Have one pound hard cream dough thoroughly warmed, just so you can handle it. When the batch is cold enough on the stove to handle, place the warm cream lengthwise on the center of it and completely wrap the cream up in it.

Place this on your table before your heater, spin out in long strips, have some one to mark them heavy or good. When cold, break where marked.

BOSTON CHIPS.—Three pounds of white sugar, one-half pipe cream tartar, one and one-fourth pints water; boil with a lid over it to the hard snap; pour; pull this only half as much as any other candy; for too much pulling takes out all the gloss when done; flavor it on the hook; wear your gloves, place it before your heater on the table, flatten out and spin out into thin ribbons, break off and curl them up in little piles.

Strawberry chips can be made the same way, adding a pinch of cochineal paste.

DATE OR FIG SQUARES.—Can be made by cutting them fine, scatter them thick over the greased stone, and pour over them a batch of barley square candy. Mark and cut with a knife.

PINE TREE TAR COUGH CANDY.—First have one tablespoon oil of tar dissolved in two tablespoons of alcohol.

Cook to a hard snap twenty pounds sugar (white), three quarts water, three pounds glucose; pour out; scatter over (while cooling) twenty drops of tar, two tablespoons oil of capsicum, three tablespoons oil of wintergreen; work all well into the batch (do not pull this on the hook).

Place before your heater on the table and spin it out in large round sticks. Have some one to keep them rolling until cold. Cut into sticks about three and one-half inches long. Wrap them in printed labels.

DATE AND FIG CREAMS.—Seed dates, cut a piece out of the end V shape, insert a white or pink cream ball, press it in, and stick a clove in the end; it looks like a pear.

Cut figs in strips, place the seedy side around a piece of cream dough. The hand made cream can be made into various varieties of candy to suit your fancy.

FACTORY CREAM DOUGH.—This recipe is worth twenty-five dollars to any candy maker. When the cream is first done it appears flaky and coarse; but the next morning it is fine, and the longer it sets the better it is. When made up it never gets stale or hard. Never use flour to roll out cream with when you can get the XXX lozenge sugar. Forty pounds granulated sugar, five quarts water; boil to a stiff ball; set off; add quickly twelve pounds of glucose. Do not stir. Set on the fire, let it come to a boil until you see even the scum boiled in (do not allow the glucose to cook in the sugar). Pour out, wait only until you can lay the back of your hand on the top of batch. (Never let it get colder, it is better to cream while hot than cold like other goods). Cream it with two garden hoes, or cream scrapers. Add while creaming one-fourth pint scant measure of glycerine. No need of kneading it, scrape into your tub for use. (If A sugar is used the cream is sticky.)

IMITATION HAND-MADE CHOCOLATE.—Take a suitable hand made. Make your plaster paris prints. Take a quantity of the above cream, melt in a bath, flavor and mould. Dip.

A NUMBER ONE CHOCOLATE DROP.—Moulding cream; granulated sugar, twenty pounds; water, three quarts. Boiled to a thread, set off, add three pounds of glucose dissolved; pour, let get cold. Cream, melt, add pinch of glucose to one pint simple syrup; four tablespoonfuls of glycerine. Stir. Mould.

CHEAP CHOCOLATES.—Quick work. Make a batch of the above number one. Exactly the same process. After the glucose is dissolved in the batch do not pour out, but add five pounds of the hard factory cream in pieces. Stir, flavor, melt. Set this kettle in a kettle of boiling water, have a boy to stir and watch it; do not allow it to get so thin as to simmer, only thin enough to run into your starch prints. This cream saves time and labor.

TO WORK OVER SCRAPS OF CANDY.—To thirty pounds of scraps use one gallon water; stir until it boils; set off, for it would never melt any more by boiling; continue stirring until all is dissolved. Set aside until cold. Skim off the top. This can be worked into hoar-hound or dark penny goods, pop-corn bricks, etc.

TO COOK OVER MAPLE SUGAR.—To sixty pounds broken up maple, add water (according to the hard or soft grain of the sugar) enough to dissolve. Stir until melted. If the grain was soft, add fifteen pounds granulated sugar; if the hard grain, only add that amount of C. sugar. Boil to 244 degrees by thermometer, or good ball. Take out some in porcelain sauce pan, grain until cloudy (to make quick work always have a small portion in the same sauce pan for the next stirring). Pour in moulds greased, or put in a tub of cold water.

ARTIFICIAL MAPLE SUGAR.—Dark C. sugar (driest), two pounds; water, one-third pint; butter, two ounces, melted; flavor with maple flavor; boil to a ball, cream in the pan. Pour before it gets too stiff.

MOLASSES POP-CORN BALLS.—Always sift your corn after it is popped. For home use, add butter and lemon flavor to your syrup. This is too expensive for retail and factory use, though some use lard sparingly. Boil molasses to a stiff ball, wet your tub, put in your corn; now with a dipper pour over your candy and stir with a paddle through the corn, wet your hands in cold water, make your balls and wrap in wax paper, twisting the ends close to the balls.

FOR WHITE OR RED.—Sugar and glucose half and half, water, to melt and boil as above. Work the same.

To make six hundred bricks a day and pop this corn, put a coarse sieve in a box or barrel bottom, instead of the natural bottom. Sift your corn. Have your popper made with a swinging wire, hanging from the ceiling down over the furnace to save labor. Have a stout, thick, wide board for the floor of your press; make a stout frame the width that two brick will measure in length; as long as twelve bricks are thick, and have your boards six or eight inches wide. Put your frame together; now make a stout lid of one-inch lumber to fit in your frame; have four cleats nailed crosswise to make it stout, and a 2×4 piece nailed lengthwise across the top of these (shorter than the lid is); now for a lever get a hard 2×4, six to eight feet long; fasten the ends of this lever to the floor, giving it six inches of the rope to play in.

Now you are ready; wet your flour board and dust it with flour; do the lid and frame the same. To every thirty pounds melted scraps of candy use two pounds of butter. (You can't cut the bricks without it.) Cook to a hard ball.

To three-fourths tub of corn, pour three small dippers of syrup; pour this when mixed in your frame on the flour board, put on the lid, with the lever press once the center, once each end, and once more the center; take out the lid, lift the frame, dump out on the table. When two-thirds cool, cut lengthwise with a sharp, thin knife, then cut your bricks off crosswise.

Penny pop-corn bricks are made the same way.

CANDY PENNY POP-CORN PIECES.—Cook a batch of glucose to a light snap, flavor well, pour thin. While hot place your pop-corn sheet hard down on the candy, mark deep cut and wrap. I have put boys on this work in the shop at five dollars a week pay, and knew them to clear for the proprietor from five to twenty dollars daily for several months; one to pop corn, one to cook syrup, one to press, and one to cut them, girls to wrap and box.

TO SHELL COCOANUTS.—Take the nut in the left hand with the three eyes up; strike from the nut down with your hatchet; peel with a knife or spoke shave, cut them into four pieces, cover them with water, set on the furnace, and let come to a good boil. If the nuts are sour, strain and add fresh cold water quickly so as the heat will not darken them, and repeat. If very sour scrape the insides out. Grate them, taking out one pieces at a time, as the air does them no good.

RED CENTER.—Take two-thirds, pour thin; color the remaining one-third red with the liquor color; place this on the half of the two-thirds, and turn the other up over on top, roll out flat with a roller, cool, cut.

The same goods cooked to a soft ball may be made into balls to be coated in red sugar after throwing them in hot sugar syrup; also to be dipped in melted cream, or brown the cocoanut balls on top with burnt sugar. Chocolate glaze cream coating eats well over these goods, or dip the balls as you like.

FLAVORINGS.—To any kind of oils take eight times in bulk the amount of Alcohol: stir, let set in a warm place a short time; can be used if needed immediately.

HOME MADE MAPLE SUGAR.—To two pounds of maple (bricks, not cakes) 1 pint water, one-third pipe cream of tartar (or four ounces of glucose is best); boil slow to a smooth degree, cool, skim. White sugar can be used.

To keep molasses from sugaring in the barrel; when making the molasses, to every barrel add twenty pounds of glucose, stir it in.

To lighten the color and aid the flavor of rank, dark molasses, do the same as above. To allow molasses to cool slowly makes it dark. It should be stirred lively until cool.

Also to improve sour, rank molasses, take the molasses, for instance, ten gallons; take five pounds dry C sugar, five pounds glucose, water two quarts. Boil the sugar and glucose until thoroughly dissolved; add the molasses, boil five minutes. You can make fine syrup this way.

TO MAKE A CANDY HOUSE.—House for a show window. Take any design you fancy, of card board. Cut out the windows; place this on your candy slab. Now with a lead pencil mark out your design, and as many of each piece as you need (it is a good idea to make an extra piece so if you break one you can go ahead). Now take of the icing sugar and fill your paper funnel as if for cake icing, and overline the pencil marks you made on the stone. When done you find you have a frame that will hold hot candy. Boil a batch of Barley Square goods (mentioned in this book), and pour on some in a dipper; take this and pour in your icing sugar frame or patterns you made on the stone, when half cold, so as not to run; run a thin knife under them carefully, lift them and lay them in a different place on the stone; when you have moulded all cut off the icing sugar that sticks to the candy. Then put your candy house together, sides first, and take pieces of lemon stick candy, dip them in the hot candy, and stick in the bottom and top corners of your house; hold them a few seconds to cool, then finish likewise. When done, take your icing sugar and funnel paper and on the outside corners of the candy house put icing sugar and the windows finish the same. Candies, if desired, can be stuck on with the icing sugar, etc. The icing sugar should be stiff for a nice job, and will hide the corners.

Candy pyramids can be made this way also.

TO MAKE A DELICIOUS CANDY COCOANUT CAKE.—Have your cake layers cold. Place in your rice steamer one-half grated cocoanut and a chunk of hand-made cream the size of your fist; stir until mixed and you can spread it; do not melt it more than necessary. This cake will not dry out if made with factory cream. I gave this recipe to two London practical cake bakers; they said it beat any cake recipe they had ever received.

Put your mind to work and with a little practice you will get up candies of your own invention, from the knowledge you derive here in this book.

ICE CREAM.—I will give only the best recipe, my own improvement, as workmen will find all my private recipes in this book to be different from others, as well as first-class. Two quarts thick cream, one pound A sugar, one-fourth ounce French gelatine, yolks of three eggs; add one quart of the cream and gelatine, set on the fire; stir; do not let boil; melt; set off, add the eggs and sugar stirred up together with a little of the cream, stirring all the time; set on, let get hot; set off, add the other quart of cream; stir, strain, freeze. Break your ice fine; use salt from one pint to one quart. Flavor after it is frozen.

FAIR GROUND LEMONADE.—Take one barrel water; dissolve in one quart of warm water twenty-five cents worth citric acid; dissolve two dollars' worth A sugar in one gallon water. Stir all together. A few cut up pieces of lemon can be added for appearance sake.

JAP COCOANUT.—One pound XXX confectioner's sugar, dampened a little; one and one-half pounds glucose; stir when cooked to a soft ball; add all the grated cocoanut it will stick together; boil, stir to the lightest crack.

LEMON ICE.—Seven lemons, the juice only, juice of three oranges. Take one pint water, dissolve in one-half ounce of French sheet gelatine; then add whites of two eggs, one and one-fourth pounds A sugar, dissolved; add all together with three pints cold water; freeze as for ice cream. Keep machine running briskly until finished.

ORANGE ICE.—The same by changing the fruit proportionately.

THE ADULTERATIONS USED BY CERTAIN FACTORIES.—(Please never try to make use of the following, for I never would print it for that purpose, only to expose the stuff.)

Grape sugar, which looks like cheap suet melted, and is so hard as to be chopped with an ax, though it dissolves readily. Terra alba, white clay, which is fine as sugar, and is sieved into cream work or on candy, and worked into it. Rice flour, ground rice mixed into cocoanut goods; cerealine, ground, prepared corn mixed into cocoanut. Glucose has the name of being an adulteration, though I fail, from seventeen years' experience, to find it such; it contains nothing outside of the acid to make it so, and that is in so small a portion as to be harmless. It is an article that is of greater value to man than the inexperienced give it credit for. If I had time I could argue this question satisfactorily to any unprejudiced person. Gamboge is a bad article for candy, yellow, cheap, hurtful color. Ground cocoanut shells are used mostly in adulterating pepper, etc. "Who is to blame for adulterating goods?" I claim three parties—first, the proprietor; next, candy makers; and next, the ignorant class of people that want sixteen cents' worth of boiled sugar for eight cents, when they do not stop to think it could not possibly be made for less than eight cents, all told.

Germany and France have strong laws against all adulterations. Soon America will prohibit the same, and bless God when the day and law we so much need will come.

HOW TO ORNAMENT CAKES.—You need four cups of confectioners' finest sugar, whites of two eggs. Beat the eggs just a little, add the sugar gradually, juice one lemon; beat this stiff, until the sugar will bend when you hold the paddle up. Now take a sheet of thick writing paper, fold it into a funnel shape, hold it in your left hand; fill this with the icing, prepared as above, about two-thirds full, fold in the top and place both thumbs on it, cut off a little of the small end of the funnel to allow the icing to come out when you press with your thumbs. Next, with a knife, cover your cake with icing sugar smoothly; if it sticks to the knife, wet it a little. Let dry half hour; then with a lead pencil make leaves or designs, and with your paper funnel ice your pencil designs. Colored icing looks well.

TAKING LEAF PHOTOGRAPHS—A very pretty amusement, especially for those who have just completed the study of botany, is the taking of leaf photographs. One very simple process is this: At any druggist's get an ounce of Bichromate of Potassium. Put this into a pint bottle of water. When the solution becomes saturated—that is, the water is dissolved as much as it will—pour off some of the clear liquid into a shallow dish; on this float a piece of ordinary writing paper till it is thoroughly moistened, let it dry in the dark. It should be a bright yellow. On this put the leaf, under a piece of black soft cloth and several sheets of newspaper. Put these between two pieces of glass (all the pieces should be of the same size) and with spring clothespins fasten them together. Expose to a bright sun, placing the leaf so that the rays will fall upon it as nearly perpendicular as possible. In a few moments it will begin to turn brown; but it requires from half an hour to several hours to produce a perfect print. When it has become dark enough, take it from the frame, and put it into clear water, which must be changed every few minutes until the yellow part becomes white. Sometimes the leaf veinings will be quite distinct. By following these directions it is scarcely possible to fail, and a little practice will make perfect.

CURIOUS THINGS.—1. To apparently burn water, fill a glass lamp with water, and put into it for a wick a piece of Gum Camphor. The lamp should not be quite full, and the camphor may be left to float upon the surface of the water. On touching a lighted match to the Camphor, up shoots a clear, steady flame, and seems to sink below the surface of the water, so that the flame is surrounded by the liquid. It will burn a long time. If the Camphor be ignited in a large dish of water it will commonly float about while burning.

2. To change the faces of a group to a livid, deathly whiteness, and to destroy colors, wet a half teacupful of common salt in Alcohol and burn it on a plate in a dark room. Let the salt soak a few minutes before igniting. The flame will deaden the brightest colors in the room, and the dresses of the company will seem to be changed. Let each one put his face behind the flame, and it will present a most ghastly spectacle to those who stand before it. This is serviceable in tableau where terror of death is to be represented. The change wrought by the flame, when the materials are properly prepared, is very surprising.

3. Wet a piece of thick wrapping paper, then dry near the stove. While dry, lay it down upon a varnished table or dry woolen cloth, and rub it briskly with a piece of India rubber. It will soon become electrified, and if tossed against the wall or the looking glass will stick some time. Tear tissue-paper into bits, one-eighth of an inch square, and this piece of electrified paper will draw them. Or take a tea-tray and put it on three tumblers. Lay the electric paper on it, and on touching the tray you will get a little spark. Let the paper lay on the tray, and on touching the tray again you will get another spark, but of the opposite kind of electricity. Replace the paper and you will get another, and so on.

4. To produce a spectrum, burn magnesium wire in a dark room, and as soon as the flame is extinguished, let each one try to look into the other's faces. The spectrum of the extinguished light is clearly seen.

MURIATE OF TIN. TIN LIQUOR.—If druggists keep it, it is best to purchase of them already made, but if you prefer, proceed as follows: Get at a tinner's shop block tin, put it into a shovel and melt it. After it is melted, pour it from the height of four or five feet into a pail of clear water. The object of this is to have the tin in small particles, so that the Acid can dissolve it. Take it out of the water and dry it; then put it in a strong brass bottle. Pour over it Muriatic Acid twelve ounces, then slowly add sulphuric acid eight ounces. The Acid should be added about a tablespoonful at a time, at intervals of five or eight minutes, for if you add it too rapidly you run the risk of breaking the bottle by heat. After you have all the Acid in, let the bottle stand until the ebullition subsides; then stop it up with beeswax or glass stopper, and set it away; and it will keep good for a year or more, or it will be fit for use in twenty-four hours.

THE CENTENNIAL ILLUMINATING OIL.—*Recipe for Making One Gallon.*—Take seven-eighths gallon Benzine or crude Petroleum, add to it one-half ounce Gum Camphor, one-half ounce Alcohol, one-half pint common Salt, one-half ounce Oil of Sassafras. Stir and mix it well for about five minutes. Let is stand for twenty-four hours and it is ready for use. It is better to buy the Benzine from Pittsburgh, Pa., as the druggists usually charge two or three times the wholesale price.

# CHAPTER X.

## COIN DEPARTMENT.

Complete and standard list of American silver and copper coins which command a premium:

**UNITED STATES SILVER DOLLARS.**

**LIBERTY 1794**

| | |
|---|---|
| 1794 Flowing Hair | $ 20 00 |
| 1794 Flowing Hair, Fine | 30 00 |
| 1795 Flowing Hair | 1 25 |
| 1796 Fillet Head | 1 25 |
| 1796 Fillet Head | 1 60 |
| 1797 Fillet Head, 6 Stars Facing | 1 60 |
| 1797 Fillet Head, 7 Stars Facing | 1 60 |
| 1798 Fillet Head, 13 Stars, Small Eagle | 1 50 |
| 1798 Fillet Head, 15 Stars, Small Eagle | 2 00 |
| 1798 13 Stars, Large Eagle | 1 10 |
| 1799 5 Stars Facing | 1 40 |
| 1799 6 Stars Facing | 1 10 |
| 1800 Spread Eagle | 1 15 |
| 1801 Spread Eagle | 1 30 |
| 1802 Spread Eagle | 1 30 |

1802  over 1801, Spread Eagle    1 35
1803  Spread Eagle               1 35

## 1804 DOLLAR.

1804  Excessively Rare           $500 00
1840  Liberty Seated             1 05
1841  Liberty Seated             1 05
1844  Liberty Seated             1 05
1845  Liberty Seated             1 05
1848  Liberty Seated             1 15
1849  Liberty Seated             1 05
1851  Liberty Seated             23 00
1852  Liberty Seated             23 00
1853  Liberty Seated             1 10
1854  Liberty Seated             2 50
1855  Liberty Seated             1 60
1856  Liberty Seated             1 50

| | | |
|---|---|---|
| 1857 | Liberty Seated | 1 50 |
| 1858 | Liberty Seated | 23 00 |
| 1861 | Liberty Seated | 1 05 |
| 1862 | Liberty Seated | 1 05 |
| 1863 | Liberty Seated | 1 05 |
| 1864 | Liberty Seated | 1 05 |
| 1865 | Liberty Seated | 1 05 |
| 1866 | Liberty Seated | 1 05 |
| 1867 | Liberty Seated | 1 05 |
| 1868 | Liberty Seated | 1 05 |
| 1869 | Liberty Seated | 1 05 |
| 1879 | Trade Dollar | 1 05 |
| 1880 | Trade Dollar | 1 05 |
| 1881 | Trade Dollar | 1 05 |
| 1882 | Trade Dollar | 1 05 |
| 1883 | Trade Dollar | 1 05 |
| 1884 | Trade Dollar | 1 05 |

**UNITED STATES PATTERN DOLLARS.**

## 1836

| | |
|---|---|
| 1836 C. Gobrecht's Name in Field | $ 9 00 |
| 1836 Flying Eagle | 4 00 |
| 1838 Flying Eagle | 17 00 |
| 1839 Flying Eagle | 13 50 |

## HALF DOLLARS.

## LIBERTY 1794

| | |
|---|---|
| 1794 Flowing Hair, Fair | $ 2 00 |
| 1794 Flowing Hair, Good | 3 00 |
| 1795 Flowing Hair | 60 |
| 1796 Fillet Head, 15 Stars | 17 50 |
| 1796 Fillet Head, 16 Stars | 20 00 |
| 1797 Fillet Head, 15 Stars | 18 00 |
| 1801 Fillet Head | 2 00 |
| 1802 Fillet Head | 2 00 |
| 1803 Fillet Head | 55 |

| | | |
|---|---|---|
| 1804 | Fillet Head | 7 50 |
| 1805 | Fillet Head | 55 |
| 1805 | over 1804, Fillet Head | 60 |
| 1806 | Fillet Head, if Extra Fine | 55 |
| 1807 | Fillet Head, if Extra Fine | 55 |
| 1807 | Head to Left, if Extra Fine | 55 |
| 1815 | Head to Left, Fair | 1 50 |
| 1815 | Head to Left, Good | 2 00 |
| 1815 | Head to Left, Fine | 2 50 |
| 1820 | over 1819 | 55 |
| 1836 | Liberty Cap, Milled Edge | 1 50 |
| 1836 | Liberty Cap, Milled Edge, Fine | 1 75 |

| | | |
|---|---|---|
| 1838 | Liberty Cap | $12 00 |

(Having "O" mark underneath bust, and meaning New Orleans Mint, under head like above cut. Ordinary 1838 half dollars without this mint mark are not wanted.)

| | | |
|---|---|---|
| 1851 | Liberty Seated | $ 55 |
| 1851 | Liberty Seated, Fine | 65 |
| 1852 | Liberty Seated, Fair | 1 40 |

| | | |
|---|---|---|
| 1852 Liberty Seated, Good | 1 75 | |
| 1852 Liberty Seated, Fine | 2 00 | |
| 1879 Liberty Seated, Fine | 55 | |

## QUARTER DOLLARS.

**LIBERTY 1796**

| | | |
|---|---|---|
| 1796 Fillet Head, Fair | $ | 1 50 |
| 1796 Fillet Head, Good | | 2 00 |
| 1804 Fillet Head, Fair | | 1 50 |
| 1804 Fillet Head, Good | | 2 00 |
| 1805 Fillet Head, Good | | 30 |
| 1806 Fillet Head, Good | | 30 |
| 1807 Head to Left | | 30 |
| 1815 Head to Left, Fine | | 35 |
| 1818 Head to Left, Fine | | 30 |
| 1819 Head to Left, Fine | | 30 |
| 1820 Head to Left, Fine | | 30 |
| 1821 Head to Left, Fine | | 30 |
| 1822 Head to Left, Fine | | 30 |
| 1823 Head to Left, Fair | | 16 00 |

| | | |
|---|---|---|
| 1823 | Head to Left, Good | 21 00 |
| 1824 | Head to Left, Fair | 35 |
| 1824 | Head to Left, Good | 60 |
| 1824 | Head to Left, Fine | 1 00 |
| 1827 | Head to Left, Fair | 17 50 |
| 1827 | Head to Left, Good | 22 00 |
| 1853 | (without Arrows and Rays) | 2 50 |

## TWENTY CENT PIECES.

| | |
|---|---|
| 1876 | $  25 |
| 1877 | 1 75 |
| 1878 | 1 75 |

## DIMES.

| | | |
|---|---|---|
| 1796 | Fillet Head, Fair | $  75 |
| 1796 | Fillet Head, Good | 1 50 |
| 1797 | 13 Stars, Fair | 1 10 |
| 1797 | 13 Stars, Good | 2 00 |
| 1797 | 16 Stars, Fair | 1 25 |
| 1796 | 16 Stars, Good | 2 00 |
| 1798 | Fillet Head, Fair | 90 |
| 1798 | Fillet Head, Good | 1 75 |

| | | |
|---|---|---:|
| 1800 | Fillet Head, Fair | 1 00 |
| 1800 | Fillet Head, Good | 1 75 |
| 1801 | Fillet Head, Fair | 1 00 |
| 1801 | Fillet Head, Good | 1 75 |
| 1802 | Fillet Head, Fair | 1 25 |
| 1802 | Fillet Head, Good | 2 00 |
| 1803 | Fillet Head, Fair | 75 |
| 1803 | Fillet Head, Good | 1 25 |
| 1804 | Fillet Head, Fair | 1 25 |
| 1804 | Filled Head, Good | 2 22 |
| 1805 | Filled Head, Good | 20 |
| 1807 | Filled Head, Good | 25 |
| 1809 | Head to Left, Fair | 20 |
| 1809 | Head to Left, Good | 50 |
| 1809 | Head to Left, Fine | 75 |
| 1811 | Head to Left, Fair | 25 |
| 1811 | Head to Left, Good | 50 |
| 1811 | Head to Left, Fine | 75 |
| 1814 | Head to Left, Fine | 15 |
| 1820 | Head to Left | 15 |
| 1821 | Head to Left, Small Date, Fine | 15 |
| 1822 | Head to Left, Fair | 50 |
| 1822 | Head to Left, Good | 75 |
| 1822 | Head to Left, Fine | 1 00 |
| 1824 | Head to Left | 15 |
| 1828 | Head to Left | 15 |

1846  Liberty Seated                $  25

## HALF DIMES.

| | | |
|---|---|---:|
| 1794 | Flowing Hair, Fair | $ 1 10 |
| 1794 | Flowing Hair, Good | 2 00 |
| 1794 | Flowing Hair, Fine | 3 00 |
| 1795 | Flowing Hair, Fair | 30 |
| 1795 | Flowing Hair, Good | 60 |
| 1796 | 15 Stars, Fillet Head, Fair | 1 50 |
| 1796 | 15 Stars, Fillet Head, Good | 2 00 |
| 1797 | 15 Stars, Fillet Head, Fair | 1 10 |
| 1797 | 15 Stars, Fillet Head, Good | 1 75 |
| 1797 | 16 Stars, Fillet Head, Fair | 1 00 |
| 1797 | 16 Stars, Fillet Head, Good | 1 75 |
| 1800 | Fillet Head, Fair | 40 |

| | | |
|---|---|---|
| 1800 | Fillet Head, Good | 75 |
| 1801 | Fillet Head, Fair | 1 00 |
| 1801 | Fillet Head, Good | 2 00 |
| 1802 | Fillet Head, Fair | 20 00 |
| 1802 | Fillet Head, Good | 40 00 |
| 1802 | Fillet Head, Fine | 75 00 |
| 1803 | Fillet Head, Fair | 1 00 |
| 1803 | Fillet Head, Good | 1 75 |
| 1805 | Fillet Head, Fair | 1 60 |
| 1805 | Fillet Head, Good | 2 25 |
| 1838 | Liberty Seated, without stars, Fair | 08 |
| 1838 | Liberty Seated, without stars, Good | 20 |
| 1838 | Liberty Seated, without stars, Fine | 30 |
| 1846 | Liberty Seated, Fair | 75 |
| 1846 | Liberty Seated, Good | 1 00 |
| 1846 | Liberty Seated, Fine | 1 50 |

## SILVER THREE CENT PIECES.

| | | |
|---|---|---|
| 1855 | Large Star in Center | $ 10 |
| 1863 | Large Star in Center | 40 |
| 1864 | Large Star in Center | 50 |
| 1865 | Large Star in Center | 30 |
| 1866 | Large Star in Center | 30 |

| | |
|---|---|
| 1867  Large Star in Center | 30 |
| 1868  Large Star in Center | 30 |
| 1869  Large Star in Center | 25 |
| 1870  Large Star in Center | 20 |
| 1871  Large Star in Center | 20 |
| 1872  Large Star in Center | 20 |
| 1873  Large Star in Center | 75 |

## NICKEL, FIVE CENT PIECES.

| | |
|---|---|
| 1877 | $ 25 |

## NICKEL, THREE CENT PIECES.

| | |
|---|---|
| 1877 | $ 40 |

## COPPER TWO CENT PIECES.

| | |
|---|---|
| 1872 | $ 05 |
| 1873 | 90 |

## COPPER CENTS.

| | | |
|---|---|---|
| 1793 Liberty Cap | $ | 1 25 |
| 1794 | | 15 |
| 1795 Liberty Cap | | 10 |
| 1796 Liberty Cap | | 15 |
| 1796 Fillet Head | | 15 |
| 1797 Fillet Head | | 08 |
| 1798 Fillet Head | | 05 |
| 1799 Fillet Head | | 3 00 |
| 1799 Fillet Head | | 6 00 |
| 1800 Fillet Head | | 05 |
| 1801 Fillet Head | | 05 |
| 1804 Fillet Head | | 2 00 |
| 1804 Fillet Head, Fine | | 2 75 |
| 1805 Fillet Head | | 08 |
| 1806 Fillet Head | | 06 |
| 1807 Fillet Head | | 03 |

| | |
|---|---|
| 1808 Head to Left | $ 10 |
| 1809 Head to Left | 40 |
| 1809 Head to Left, Fine | 75 |
| 1810 Head to Left | 05 |
| 1811 Head to Left | 25 |
| 1812 Head to Left | 03 |
| 1813 Head to Left | 15 |
| 1814 Head to Left | 05 |
| 1817 Head to Left, 15 Stars | 05 |
| 1821 Head to Left | 08 |
| 1823 Head to Left | 12 |
| 1857 Head to Left, Large Date | 06 |
| 1857 Head to Left | 06 |
| 1857 Head to Left, Small Date | 06 |

**EAGLE NICKEL CENTS.**

| | | |
|---|---|---|
| 1856 | Fair | $ 55 |
| 1856 | Good | 80 |
| 1856 | Fine | 1 10 |

## HALF CENTS.

| | | |
|---|---|---|
| 1793 | Liberty Cap | $ 1 00 |
| 1794 | Liberty Cap | 25 |
| 1795 | Lettered Edge | 20 |
| 1795 | Thin Die | 20 |
| 1796 | Liberty Cap | 7 50 |
| 1797 | Liberty Cap | 25 |
| 1797 | Lettered Edge | 85 |
| 1800 | Fillet Head | 05 |
| 1802 | Fillet Head | 60 |
| 1803 | Fillet Head | 05 |
| 1805 | Fillet Head | 06 |
| 1806 | Fillet Head | 06 |
| 1807 | Fillet Head | 06 |
| 1808 | Fillet Head | 06 |
| 1810 | Head to Left | 18 |
| 1811 | Head to Left | 60 |
| 1831 | Head to Left | 2 00 |

| | | |
|---|---|---|
| 1836 | Head to Left | 3 00 |
| 1840 | Head to Left | 1 75 |
| 1841 | Head to Left | 1 75 |
| 1842 | Head to Left | 2 50 |
| 1843 | Head to Left | 3 00 |
| 1844 | Head to Left | 2 00 |
| 1845 | Head to Left | 1 75 |
| 1846 | Head to Left | 1 75 |
| 1847 | Head to Left | 2 50 |
| 1848 | Head to Left | 3 00 |
| 1849 | Head to Left, Small Date | 3 00 |
| 1849 | Head to Left, Large Date | 06 |
| 1850 | Head to Left | 05 |
| 1852 | Head to Left | 2 50 |
| 1854 | Head to Left | 05 |
| 1856 | Head to Left | 15 |
| 1857 | Head to Left | 08 |

## AMERICAN SILVER AND COPPER COINS NOT ISSUED BY THE UNITED STATES MINT.

### SILVER COINAGE.

DOLLARS.—First coinage, 1794; none issued 1805 to 1835, inclusive, and 1837.

HALF-DOLLARS.—First coinage, 1794; none issued 1798, 1799, 1816.

QUARTER-DOLLARS.—First coinage, 1796; none issued 1794, 1795, 1797 to 1804, 1808 to 1814, inclusive, 1816, 1817, 1826, 1829, 1830.

DIMES.—First coinage, 1796; none issued 1794, 1795, 1799, 1806, 1808, 1810, 1812, 1813, 1815 to 1819, inclusive, 1826.

HALF-DIMES.—First coinage, 1794; none issued 1798, 1799, 1801, 1806 to 1828, inclusive. The coinage of half-dimes was discontinued in 1873 by Act of Congress.

THREE-CENT PIECES (SILVER).—First coinage, 1851; and then the dates follow in succession until 1873, when the coinage of them was discontinued.

## COPPER CENTS.

COPPER CENTS.—First coinage, 1793, none issued 1815; they then follow to 1857, when the coinage was changed to nickel. The nickel cent of 1856 was only a pattern, which continued during this year up to 1864, inclusive. The bronze cent was introduced in this year. In 1865 the nickel cent was discontinued, and up to date the bronze cents are issued.

HALF-CENTS.—First coinage, 1793; none issued 1798, 1799, 1801, 1812 to 1824, inclusive; 1827, 1837, 1838, 1839; in 1857 the issue of half-cents was discontinued.

In 1864 the two-cent piece in bronze was introduced, and discontinued in 1873, by Act of Congress.

In 1865 the three-cent nickel piece was first issued.

In 1866 the five-cent piece was first issued; a very few were struck in 1865 as pattern. In 1883 the die was changed to that of the current issue with liberty head. Although upwards of five million coins of the 1883 nickels without the words "cents" were issued, they will in the course of a few years command a premium. At present they are still quite common.

## LOISETTE'S SYSTEM OF MEMORY.

So much has been said about Loisette's memory system, the art has been so widely advertised, and so carefully guarded from all the profane who do not send five or many dollars to the professor, that a few pages showing how every man may be his own Loisette, may be both interesting and valuable.

In the first place, the system is a good one, and well worth the labor of mastering, and if the directions are implicitly followed there can be no doubt that the memory will be greatly strengthened and improved, and that mnemonic feats, otherwise impossible, may be easily performed. Loisette, however, is not an inventor, but an introducer. He stands in the same relation to Dr. Pick that the retail dealer holds to the manufacturer; the one produced the article; the other brings it to the public. Even this statement is not quite fair to Loisette, for he has brought much practical common sense to bear upon Pick's system, and in preparing the new art of mnemonics for the market, in many ways he has made it his own.

If each man would reflect upon the method by which he himself remembers things, he would find his hand upon the key of the whole mystery. For instance, the author was once trying to remember the word *blythe*. There occurred to my mind the words "Bellman," "Belle," and then the verse

>—the peasant upward climbing
>Hears the bells of *Buloss* chiming.

"Barcarole," "Barrack," and so on, until the word "blythe" presented itself with a strange insistence, long after I had ceased trying to recall it.

On another occasion, when trying to recall the name "Richardson," I got the words "hay-rick," "Robertson," "Randallstown," and finally "wealthy," from which naturally I got "rich" and "Richardson" almost in a breath.

Still another example: trying to recall the name of an old schoolmate, "Grady," I got "Brady," "grave," "gaseous," "gastronome," "gracious," and I finally abandoned the attempt, simply saying to myself that it began with a "G," and there was an "a" sound after it. The next morning, when thinking of something entirely different, this name "Grady" came up in my mind with as much distinctness as though some one had whispered it in my ear. This remembering was done without any conscious effort on my part, and was evidently the result of the exertion made the day before, when mnemonic processes were put to work. Every reader must have had similar experience, which he can recall, and which will fall in line with the examples given.

It follows, then, that when we endeavor, without the aid of any system, to recall a forgotten fact or name, our memory presents to us words of a similar sound or meaning in its journey toward the goal to which we have started it. This goes to show that our ideas are arranged in groups in whatever secret cavity or recess of the brain they occupy, and that the arrangement is one not alphabetical exactly and not entirely by meaning, but after some fashion partaking of both.

If you are looking for the word "meadow" you may reach "middle" before you come to it, or "Mexico," or many words beginning with the "m" sound, or containing the "dow," as "window" or "dough," or you may get "field" or "farm"—but you are on the right track, and if you do not interfere with your intellectual process you will finally come to the idea which you are seeking.

How often have you heard people say: "I forget his name; it is something like Beadle or Beagle—at any rate it begins with a B." Each and all of these were unconscious Loisettians, and they were practicing blindly, and without proper method or direction, the excellent system which he teaches. The thing, then, to do—and it is the final and simple truth which Loisette teaches—is to travel over this ground in the other direction—to cement the fact which you wish to remember to some other fact or word which you know will be brought out by the implied conditions—and thus you will always be able to travel from your given starting point to the thing which you wish to call to mind.

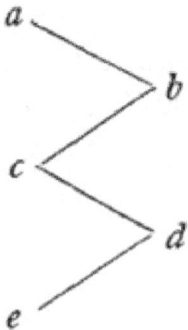

To illustrate: let the broken line in the annexed diagram represent a train of thought. If we connect the idea "a" with "e" through the steps b, c and d, the tendency of the mind ever afterward will be to get to e from a that way, or from any of the intermediates that way. It seems as though a channel were cut in our mindstuff along which the memory flows. How to make it flow this way will be seen later on. Loisette, in common with all mnemonic teachers, uses the old devise of representing numbers by letter—and as this is the first and easiest step in the art, this seems to be the most logical place to introduce the accepted equivalents of the Arabic numerals:

0 is always represented by *s, z* or *c* soft.

1 is always represented by *t, th* or *d*.

2 is always represented by *n*.

3 is always represented by *m*.

4 is always represented by *r*.

5 is always represented by *l*.

6 is always represented by *sh, j, ch* soft or *g* soft.

7 is always represented by *g* hard, *kc* hard, *q* or final *ng*.

8 is always represented by *f* or *v*.

9 is always represented by *p* or *b*.

All the other letters are used simply to fill up. Double letters in a word count only as one. In fact, the system goes by sound, not by spelling—for instance, "this" or "dizzy" would stand for *ten*; "catch" or "gush" would stand for 76, and the only difficulty is to make some word or phrase which will contain only the significant letters in the proper order, filled out with non-significants into some guise of meaning or intelligibility.[2] Suppose you wish to get some phrase or word that would express the number 3,685, you arrange the letters this way:

|   | 3 | ∩ | 6 | ∩ | 8 | ∩ | 5 |
|---|---|---|---|---|---|---|---|
| a | m | a | sh | a | f | a | l |
| e |   | e | j | e | v | e |   |
| i |   | i | ch | i |   | i |   |
| o |   | o | g | o |   | o |   |
| u |   | u |   | u |   | u |   |
| h |   | h |   | h |   | h |   |
| w |   | w |   | w |   | w |   |
| x |   | x |   | x |   | x |   |
| y |   | y |   | y |   | y |   |

You can make out "image of law," "my shuffle," "matchville," etc., etc., as far as you like to work it out.

Now, suppose you wish to memorize the fact that $1,000,000 in gold weighs 3,685 pounds, you go about it in this way, and here is the kernel and crux of Loisette's system:

"How much does $1,000,000 in gold weigh?"

"Weigh—scales."

"Scales—statue of Justice."

"Statue of Justice—*image of law.*"

The process is simplicity itself. The thing you wish to recall, and that you fear to forget, is the weight; consequently you cement your chain of suggestion to the idea which is most prominent to your mental question. What do you weigh with? Scales. What does the mental picture of scales suggest? The statue of Justice, blindfolded and weighing out award and punishment to man. Finally, what is this statue of Justice but the image of law? And the words "image of law," translated back from the significant letters *m, g* soft, *f* and *l*, give you 3—6—8—5, the number of pounds in $1,000,000 in gold. You bind together in your mind each separate step in the journey, the one suggests the other, and you will find a year from now that the fact will be as fresh in your memory as it is to-day. You cannot lose it. It is chained to you by an unbreakable mnemonic tie. Mark, that it is not claimed that "weight" will of itself suggest "scales" and "scales" "statue of Justice," etc., but that, once having passed your attention up and down the ladder of ideas, your mental tendency will be to take the same route, and get to the same goal again and again. Indeed, beginning with the weight of $1,000,000, "image of law" will turn up in your mind without your consciousness of any intermediate station on the way, after some iteration and reiteration of the original chain.

Again, so as to fasten the process in the reader's mind even more firmly, suppose that it were desired to fix the date of the battle of Hastings (A.D. 1066) in the memory; 1066 may be represented by the words "the wise judge" (*th* equals 1, *s* equals 0, *j* equals 6, *dg* equals 6; the others are non-significants); a chain might be made thus:

Battle of Hastings—arbitrament of war.

Arbitrament of war—arbitration.

Arbitration—judgment.

Judgment—the wise judge.

Make mental pictures, connect ideas, repeat words and sounds, go about it in any way you please, so that you will form a mental habit of connecting the "battle of Hastings" with the idea of "arbitrament of war," and so on for the other links in the chain, and the work is done.

Loisette makes the beginning of his system unnecessarily difficult, to say nothing of his illogical arrangement in the grammar of the art of memory, which he makes the first of his lessons. He analyzes suggestion thus:

1. Inclusion. 2. Exclusion. 3. Concurrence.

All of which looks very scientific and orderly, but is really misleading and badly named. The truth is that one idea will suggest another.

1. By likeness or opposition of meaning, as "house" suggests "room" or "door," etc., or "white" suggests "blacks," "cruel," "kind," etc.

2. By likeness of sound, as "harrow" and "barrow;" "Henry" and "Hennepin."

3. By mental juxtaposition, a peculiarity different in each person and depending upon each one's own experiences. Thus "St. Charles" suggests "railway bridge" to me, because I was vividly impressed by the breaking of the Wabash bridge at that point. "Stable" and "broken leg" come near each other in my experience, so do "cow" and "shot-gun" and "licking."

Out of these three sorts of suggestions it is possible to get from any one fact to any other in a chain certain and safe, along which the mind may be depended upon afterward always to follow.

The chain is, of course, by no means all. Its making and its binding must be accompanied by a vivid, methodically directed attention, which turns all the mental light gettable in a focus upon the subject passing across the mind's screen. Before Loisette was thought of this was known. In the old times in England, in order to impress upon the minds of the rising generation the parish boundaries in the rural districts, the boys were taken to each of the landmarks in succession, the position and bearings of each pointed out carefully, and, in order to deepen the impression, the young people were then and there vigorously thrashed, a mechanical method of attracting the attention which was said never to have failed. This system has had its supporters in many of the old-fashioned schools, and there are men who will read these lines who can recall, with an itching sense of vivid expression, the 144 lickings which were said to go with the multiplication table.

In default of a thrashing, however, the student must cultivate as best he can an intense fixity of perception upon every fact or word or date that he wishes to make permanently his own. It is easy. It is a matter of habit. If you will you can photograph an idea upon your cerebral gelatine so that neither years nor events will blot it out or overlay it. You must be clearly and distinctly aware of the thing you are putting into your mental treasure-house, and drastically certain of the cord by which you have tied it to some other thing of which you are sure. Unless it is worth your while to do this, you might as well abandon any hopes of mnemonic improvement, which will not come without the hardest kind of hard work, although it is work that will grow constantly easier with practice and reiteration.

You need, then:

1. Methodic suggestion.
2. Methodic attention.
3. Methodic reiteration.

And this is all there is to Loisette, and a great deal it is. Two of them will not do without the third. You do not know how many steps there are from your hall-door to your bed-room, though you have attended to and often reiterated the journey. But if there are twenty of them, and you have once bound the word "nice," or "nose," or "news," or "hyenas," to the fact of the stairway, you could never forget it.

The Professor makes a point, and very wisely, of the importance of working through some established chain, so that the whole may be carried away in the mind—not alone for the value of the facts so bound together, but for the mental discipline so afforded.

Here, then, is the "President Series," which contains the name and the date of inauguration of each President from Washington to Cleveland. The manner in which it is to be mastered is this: Beginning at the top, try to find in your mind some connection between each word and the one following it. See how you can at some future time make one suggest the next, either by suggestion of sound or sense, or by mental juxtaposition. When you have found this dwell on it attentively for a moment or two. Pass it backward and forward before you, and then go on to the next step.

The chain runs thus, the names of the Presidents being in small caps, the date word in italics:

| | |
|---|---|
| President | Chosen as the first word as the one most apt to occur to the mind of any one wishing to repeat the names of the Presidents. |
| Dentist | Presi*dent* and *dent*ist. |
| Draw | What does a dentist do? |
| *To give up* | When something is drawn from one it is given up. This is a date phrase meaning 1789. |
| Self-sacrifice | There is an association of thought between giving and self-sacrifice. |
| WASHINGTON | Associate the quality of self-sacrifice with Washington's character. |
| Morning wash | *Wash*ington and *wash*. |
| Dew | Early witness and dew. |
| Flower beds | Dew and flowers. |
| *Took a bouquet* | Flowers and bouquet. Date phrase (1707.) |
| Garden | Bouquet and garden. |
| Eden | The first garden. |
| Adam | Juxtaposition of thought. |

| | |
|---|---|
| ADAMS | Suggestion by sound. |
| Fall | Juxtaposition by thought. |
| Failure | Fall and failure. |
| *Deficit* | Upon a failure there is usually a deficit. Date word (1801.) |
| Debt | The consequence of a deficit. |
| Bonds | Debt and bonds. |
| Confederate bonds | Suggestion by meaning. |
| Jefferson Davis | Juxtaposition of thought. |
| JEFFERSON. | |

Now, follow out the rest for yourself, taking about ten at a time, and binding those you do last to those you have done before each time, before attacking the next bunch.

| 1 | 2 | 3 |
|---|---|---|
| JEFFERSON | *the fraud* | *the heavy shell* |
| Judge Jeffreys | painted clay | mollusk |
| bloody assize | baked clay | unfamiliar word |
| bereavement | tiles | dictionary |
| *too heavy a sob* | TYLER | Johnson's |
| parental grief | Wat Tyler | JOHNSON |
| mad son | poll tax | son |
| MADISON | compulsory | bad son |
| Madeira | *free will* | dishonest boy |
| first-rate wine | free offering | *thievish boy* |
| frustrating | burnt offering | take |
| *defeating* | poker | give |
| feet | POLK | GRANT |
| toe the line | end of dance | award |
| row | termination "ly" | school premium |

| | | |
|---|---|---|
| MUNROE | *adverb* | examination |
| row | part of speech | cramming |
| boat | part of a man | *fagging* |
| steamer | TAYLOR | laborer |
| *the funnel* | measurer | hay field |
| windpipe | theodolite | HAYES |
| throat | *Theophilus* | hazy |
| quinzy | fill us | clear |
| QUINZY ADAMS | FILLMORE | *vivid* |
| quince | more fuel | brightly lighted |
| fine fruit | *the flame* | camp fire |
| *the fine boy* | flambeau | war field |
| sailor boy | bow | GARFIELD |
| sailor | arrow | Guiteau |
| jack tar | PIERCE | murderer |
| JACKSON | hurt | prisoner |
| stone wall | *feeling* | prison fare |
| indomitable | wound | *half fed* |
| *tough make* | soldier | well fed |
| oaken furniture | cannon | well read |
| bureau | BUCHANAN | author |
| VAN BUREN | rebuke | ARTHUR |
| rent | official censure | round table |
| side-splitting | *to officiate* | tea table |
| *divert* | wedding | tea cup |
| annoy | linked | *half full* |
| harrassing | LINCOLN | divide |
| HARRISON | link | cleave |
| Old Harry | stroll | CLEVELAND |
| | | |

# One Thousand Secrets of Wise and Rich Men Revealed

| the tempter | sea shore | |
|---|---|---|

It will be noted that some of the date words, as "free will," only give three figures of the date, 845; but it is to be supposed that if the student knows that many figures in the date of Polk's inauguration he can guess the other one.

The curious thing about this system will now become apparent. If the reader has learned the series so that he can say it down from first President to Cleveland, he can with no effort, and without any further preparation, say it *backward*, from Cleveland up to the commencement. There could be no better proof that this is the natural mnemonic system. It proves itself by its works.

|  |  |  |
|---|---|---|
|  | 0 —hoes |  |
| 1 —wheat | 34 —mare | 67 —jockey |
| 2 —hen | 35 —mill | 68 —shave |
| 3 —home | 36 —image | 69 —ship |
| 4 —hair | 37 —mug | 70 —eggs |
| 5 —oil | 38 —muff | 71 —gate |
| 6 —shoe | 39 —mob | 72 —gun |
| 7 —hook | 40 —race | 73 —comb |
| 8 —off | 41 —hart | 74 —hawker |
| 9 —bee | 42 —horn | 75 —coal |
| 10 —daisy | 43 —army | 76 —cage |
| 11 —tooth | 44 —warrior | 77 —cake |
| 12 —dine | 45 —royal | 78 —coffee |
| 13 —time | 46 —arch | 79 —cube |
| 14 —tower | 47 —rock | 80 —vase |
| 15 —dell | 48 —wharf | 81 —feet |
| 16 —ditch | 49 —rope | 82 —vein |
| 17 —duck | 50 —wheels | 83 —fame |
| 18 —dove | 51 —lad | 84 —fire |

C. A. Bogardus

| | | |
|---|---|---|
| 19 — tabby | 52 — lion | 85 — vial |
| 20 — hyenas | 53 — lamb | 86 — fish |
| 21 — hand | 54 — lair | 87 — fig |
| 22 — nun | 55 — lily | 88 — fife |
| 23 — name | 56 — lodge | 89 — fib |
| 24 — owner | 57 — lake | 90 — pies |
| 25 — nail | 58 — leaf | 91 — putty |
| 26 — hinge | 59 — elbow | 92 — pane |
| 27 — ink | 60 — chess | 93 — bomb |
| 28 — knife | 61 — cheat | 94 — bier |
| 29 — knob | 62 — chain | 95 — bell |
| 30 — muse | 63 — sham | 96 — peach |
| 31 — mayday | 64 — chair | 97 — book |
| 32 — hymen | 65 — jail | 98 — beef |
| 33 — mama | 66 — judge | 99 — pope |
| | 100 — diocese | |

The series should be repeated backward and forward every day for a month, and should be supplemented by a series of the reader's own making, and by this one, which gives the numbers from 0 to 100, and which must be chained together before they can be learned.

By the use of this table, which should be committed as thoroughly as the President series, so that it can be repeated backwards and forwards, any date, figure or number can be at once constructed, and bound by the usual chain to the fact which you wish it to accompany.

When the student wishes to go farther and attack larger problems than the simple binding of two facts together, there is little in Loisette's system that is new, although there is much that is good. If it is a book that is to be learned, as one would prepare for an examination, each chapter is to be considered separately. Of each a *precis* is to be written in which the writer must exercise all of his ingenuity to reduce the matter in hand to its final skeleton of fact. This he is to commit to memory both by the use of the chain and the old system of interrogation. Suppose after much labor through a wide space of language one boils a chapter to an event down to the final irreducible sediment: "Magna Charta was exacted by the barons from King John at Runnymede."

You must now turn this statement this way and that way, asking yourself about it every possible and impossible question, gravely considering the answers, and, if you find any part of it especially difficult to remember, chaining it to the question which will bring it out. Thus, "What was exacted by the barons from King John at Runnymede?" "Magna Charta." "By whom was Magna Charta exacted from King John at Runnymede?" "By the barons." "From whom was," etc., etc.? "King John." "From what king," etc., etc.? "King John." "Where was Magna Charta," etc., etc.? "At Runnymede."

And so on and so on, as long as your ingenuity can suggest questions to ask, or points of view from which to consider the statement. Your mind will be finally saturated with the information and prepared to spill it out at the first squeeze of the examiner. This, however, is not new. It was taught in the schools hundreds of years before Loisette was born. Old newspaper men will recall in connection with it Horace Greeley's statement that the test of a news item was the clear and satisfactory manner in which a report answered the interrogatories, "What?" "When?" "Where?" "Who?" "Why?"

In the same way Loisette advises the learning of poetry, *e.g.*,

> "The Assyrian came down like a wolf on the fold."

"Who came down?"

"How did the Assyrian come down?"

"Like what animal did?" etc.

And so on and so on, until the verses are exhausted of every scrap of information to be had out of them by the most assiduous cross-examination.

Whatever the reader may think of the availability or value of this part of the system, there are so many easily applicable tests of the worth of much that Loisette has done, that it may be taken with the rest.

Few people, to give an easy example, can remember the value of +— the ratio between the circumference and the diameter of the circle—beyond four places of decimals, or at most six—3,141,592+. Here is the value to 108 decimal places:

3. 14159265 · 3589793238 · 4626433832 ·7950288419 · 7169399375 · 1058209749 · 4459230781 · 6406286208 · 9986280348 · 2534211706 · 7982148086

By a very simple application of the numerical letter values these 108 decimal places can be carried in the mind and recalled about as fast as you can write them down. All that is to be done is to memorize these nonsense lines:

Mother Day will buy any shawl.
My love pick up my new muff.
A Russian jeer may move a woman.
Cables enough for Utopia.
Get a cheap ham pie by my cooley.
The slave knows a bigger ape.
I rarely hop on my sick foot.
Cheer a sage in a fashion safe.
A baby fish now views my wharf.
Annually Mary Ann did kiss a jay.
A cabby found a rough savage.

Now translate each significant into its proper value and you have the task accomplished. "Mother Day," *m* equals 3, *th* equals 1, *r* equals 4, *d* equals 1, and so on. Learn the lines one at a time by the method of interrogatories. "Who will buy any shawl?" "Which Mrs. Day will buy a shawl?" "Is Mother Day particular about the sort of shawl she will buy?" "Has she bought a shawl?" etc., etc. Then cement the end of each line to the beginning of the next one, thus, "Shawl"—"warm garment"—"warmth"—"love"—"my love," and go on as before. Stupid as the work may seem to you, you can memorize the figures in fifteen minutes this way so that you will not forget them in fifteen years. Similarly you can take Haydn's Dictionary of Dates and turn fact after fact into nonsense lines like these which you cannot lose.

And this ought to be enough to show anybody the whole art. If you look back across the sands of time and find out that it is that ridiculous old "Thirty days hath September," which comes to you when you are trying to think of the length of October—if you can quote your old prosody,

"O datur ambiguis," etc.

with much more certainty than you can serve up your Horace; if in fine, jingles and alliterations, wise and otherwise, have stayed with you, while solid and serviceable information has faded away, you may be certain that here is the key to the enigma of memory.

You can apply it yourself in a hundred ways. If you wish to clinch in your mind the fact that Mr. Love lives at 485 Dearborn Street, what is more easy than to turn 485 into the words "rifle" and chain the ideas together, say thus: "Love—happiness—good time—picnic—forest—wood rangers—range—rifle range—*rifle*—fine weapon—costly weapon—dearly bought—DEARBORN."

Or if you wish to remember Mr. Bowman's name, and you notice he has a mole on his face which is apt to attract your attention when you next see him, cement the ideas thus: "Mole, mark, target, archer, Bowman."

# FACTS WORTH KNOWING.

## HANDY FACTS TO SETTLE MANY ARGUMENTS

London plague in 1665.

Telephone invented 1861.

There are 2,750 languages.

Two persons die every second.

Sound moves 743 miles per hour.

Chinese invented paper 170 B.C.

A square mile contains 640 acres.

A barrel of pork weighs 200 pounds.

Hawks can fly 150 miles in one hour.

Watches were first constructed in 1476.

Chinese in United States in 1880, 105,613.

Rome was founded by Romulus, 752 B.C.

Gold was discovered in California in 1848.

Phonograph invented by T. A. Edison, 1877.

The first balloon ascended from Lyons, France, 1783.

The first fire insurance office in America, Boston, 1724.

Jet is found along the coast of Yorkshire, Eng., near Whitby.

Napoleon I. crowned emperor 1804; died at St. Helena, 1820.

Electric light invented by Lodyguin and Kossloff, at London, 1874.

Harvard is the oldest college in the United States: established 1638.

War declared with Great Britain, June 19, 1812; peace Feb. 18, 1815.

Until 1776 cotton spinning was performed by the hand spinning-wheel.

Measure 209 feet on each side and you will have a square acre within an inch.

Postage stamps first came into use in England in the year 1840; in the United States in 1847.

The highest range of mountains are the Himalayas, the mean elevation being from 16,000 to 18,000 feet.

Envelopes were first used in 1839.

Telescopes were invented in 1590.

Iron horseshoes were made in 481.

A barrel of flour weighs 196 pounds.

A hand (horse measure) is four inches.

A rifle ball moves 1,000 miles per hour.

First steamer crossed the Atlantic, 1819.

Assassination of Lincoln, April 14, 1865.

# One Thousand Secrets of Wise and Rich Men Revealed

German empire re-established, Jan. 18, 1871.

Storm clouds move thirty-six miles an hour.

First subscription library, Philadelphia, 1731.

Dark Ages, from the 6th to the 14th century.

The Latin tongue became obsolete about 580.

The great London fire occurred Sept. 26, 1666.

The value of a ton of pure gold is $602,799.21.

Ether was first used for surgical purposes in 1844.

Ignatius Loyola founded the order of Jesuits, 1541.

First authentic use of organs, 755; in England, 951.

The first newspaper advertisement appeared in 1652.

Cork is the bark taken from a species of the oak tree.

Benjamin Franklin used the first lightning rods, 1752.

Glass windows (colored) were used in the 8th century.

Authentic history of China commenced 3,000 years B.C.

Introduction of homœpathy into the United States, 1825.

Spectacles were invented by an Italian in the 13th century.

Medicine was introduced into Rome from Greece, 200 B.C.

First electric telegraph, Paddington to Brayton, Eng., 1835.

The Chaldeans were the first people who worked in metals.

First life insurance, in London, 1772; in America, Philadelphia, 1812.

Egyptian pottery is the oldest known; dates from 2,000 B.C.

Julius Cæsar invaded Britain, 55 B.C.; assassinated, 44 B.C.

Soap was first manufactured in England in the 16th century.

The largest free territorial government is the United States.

First photographs produced in England, 1802; perfected, 1841.

First marine insurance, A.D. 533; England, 1598; America, 1721.

Professor Oersted, Copenhagen, discovered electro-magnetism, in 1819.

First American express, New York to Boston—W. F. Harnden.

Glass windows were first introduced into England in the 8th century.

Chicago is little more than fifty years old, and is the eighteenth city of the world.

Glass was made in Egypt, 3000 B.C.; earliest date of transparent glass, 719 B.C.

First public schools in America were established in the New England States about 1642.

The largest inland sea is the Caspian, between Europe and Asia, being 700 miles long and 270 miles wide.

The term "Almighty Dollar" originated with Washington Irving, as a satire on the American love for gain.

The highest natural bridge in the world is at Rockbridge, Virginia, being 200 feet high to the bottom of the arch.

The largest circulation of paper money is that of the United States, being 700 millions, while Russia has 670 millions.

The largest insurance company in the world is the Mutual Life of New York City, having cash assets of $108,000,000.

The largest empire in the world is that of Great Britain, being 8,557,658 square miles, and more than a sixth part of the globe.

The first electrical signal ever transmitted between Europe and America passed over the Field submarine cable on Aug. 5, 1858.

The longest tunnel in the world is St. Gothard, on the line of the railroad between Luzerne and Milan, being nine and one-half miles in length.

The loftiest active volcano is Popocatapetl. It is 17,784 feet high, and has a crater three miles in circumference and 1,000 feet deep.

Burnt brick was known to have been used in building the Tower of Babel. They were introduced into England by the Romans.

The most remarkable echo known is that in the castle of Simonetta, two miles from Milan. It repeats the echo of a pistol sixty times.

The largest volcano in the world is Etna. Its base is 90 miles in circumference; its cone 11,000 feet high. Its first eruption occurred 474 B.C.

The largest tree in the world, as yet discovered, is in Tulare County, California. It is 275 feet high and 106 feet in circumference at its base.

The largest desert is Sahara, in Northern Africa. Its length is 3,000 miles and breadth 900 miles; having an area of 2,000,000 square miles.

The largest suspension bridge is in Brooklyn. The length of the main span is 1,595 feet 6 inches. The entire length of the bridge is 5,989 feet.

The first deaf and dumb asylum was founded in England by Thomas Braidwood, 1760; and the first in the United States was at Hartford, 1817.

The largest diamond in the world is the Braganza, being a part of the Portuguese jewels. It weighs 1,880 carats. It was found in Brazil in 1741.

The grade of titles in Great Britain stands in the following order from the highest: A Prince, Duke, Marquis, Earl, Viscount, Baron, Baronet, Knight.

The largest number of cattle ever received in one year was that of Chicago in the year 1884, being 1,874,984 beeves, 30,223 calves, 5,640,625 hogs, 749,917 sheep and 15,625 horses. It required 9,000 trains of 31 cars each, which, if coupled together, would reach 2,146 miles.

The "Valley of Death," in the island of Java, is simply the crater of an extinct volcano, filled with carbonic-acid gas. It is half a mile in circumference.

The city of Amsterdam, Holland, is built upon piles driven into the ground. It is intersected by numerous canals, crossed by nearly three hundred bridges.

Coal was used as fuel in England as early as 852, and in 1234 the first charter to dig for it was granted by Henry III. to the inhabitants of Newcastle-on-Tyne.

Tobacco was discovered in San Domingo in 1496; afterwards by the Spaniards in Yucatan in 1520. It was introduced in France in 1560, and into England in 1583.

The present national colors of the United States were not adopted by Congress until 1777. The flag was first used by Washington at Cambridge, January 1, 1776.

Paris was known as Lutetia until 1184, when the name of the great French capital was changed to that which it has borne ever since.

The longest span of wire in the world is used for a telegraph in India over the river Ristuah. It is over 6,000 feet, and is stretched between two hills 1,200 feet high.

The largest library in the world is in Paris, founded by Louis XIV. It contains 1,400,000 volumes, 175,000 manuscripts, 300,000 maps and charts, and 150,000 coins and medals.

The tallest man was John Hale, of Lancashire, England, who was nine feet six inches in height. His hand was seventeen inches long and eight and one-half inches broad.

In round numbers, the weight of $1,000,000 in standard gold coin is 1¾ tons; standard silver coin, 26¾ tons; subsidiary silver coin, 25 tons; minor coins, 5-cent nickel, 100 tons.

The largest stationery engine in the world is at the zinc mines at Friedenville, Pa. The number of gallons of water raised every minute is 17,500. The driving wheels are 35 feet diameter and weigh 40 tons each. The cylinder is 110 inches in diameter.

The part of United States territory most recently acquired is the island of San Juan, near Vancouver's Island. It was evacuated by England at the close of November, 1873.

The highest monument in the world is the Washington monument, being 555 feet. The highest structure of any kind is the Eiffel Tower, Paris, finished in 1889 and 989 feet high.

It is claimed that crows, eagles, ravens and swans live to be 100 years old; herons, 59; parrots, 60; pelicans and geese, 50; skylarks, 30; sparrow hawks, 40; peacocks, canaries and cranes, 24.

The greatest cataract in the world is Niagara, the height of the American falls being 165 feet. The highest fall of water in the world is that of the Yosemite in California, being 2,550 feet.

The most ancient catacombs are those of the Theban kings, begun 4,000 years ago. The catacombs of Rome contain the remains of about 6,000,000 human beings; those of Paris, 3,000,000.

The quickest passage ever made across the Atlantic was that of the steamer Lucania, of the Cunard line, being 5 days 7 hours and 23 minutes from New York to Queenstown; the distance being 2,850 miles.

There has been no irregularity in the recurrence of leap year every four years since 1800, and will be none until 1900, which will be a common year, although it will come fourth after the preceding leap year.

The first English newspaper was the *English Mercury*, issued in the reign of Queen Elizabeth, and was issued in the shape of a pamphlet. The *Gazette* of Venice was the original model of the modern newspaper.

The Mormon Church in Utah shows a membership of 127,294—23,000 families. The church has 12 apostles, 58 patriarchs, 3,885 seventies, 3,153 high priests, 11,000 elders, 1,500 bishops and 4,400 deacons, being an office for each six persons.

A "monkey wrench" is not so named because it is a handy thing to monkey with, or for any kindred reason. "Monkey" is not its name at all, but "Moncky." Charles Moncky, the inventor of it, sold his patent for $2,000, and invested the money in a house in Williamsburg, King's County, N.Y., where he now lives.

The Union arch of the Washington Aqueduct is the largest in the world, being 220 feet; 20 feet in excess of the Chester arch across the Dee in England, 68 feet longer than that of the London bridge; 92 feet longer than that at Neuilly on the Seine, and 100 feet longer than that of Waterloo bridge. The height of the Washington arch is 100 feet.

The largest ship ever built, the Great Eastern, recently broken to pieces and sold to junk dealers, was designed and constructed by Scott Russell, at Maxwell, on the Thames. Work on the giant vessel was commenced in May,

1854. She was successfully launched January 13, 1858. The launching alone occupied the time from November 3, 1857, until the date above given. Her total length was 600 feet; breadth, 118 feet; total weight when launched 12,000 tons. Her first trip of any consequence was made to New York in 1859-60.

The most extensive mines in the world are those of Freiberg, Saxony. They were begun in the twelfth century, and in 1835 the galleries, taken collectively, had reached the unprecedented length of 123 miles. A new gallery, begun in 1838, had reached a length of eight miles at the time of the census of 1878. The deepest perpendicular mining shaft in the world is located at Prizilram, Bohemia. It is a lead mine; it was begun 1832. January, 1880, it was 3,280 feet deep. The deepest coal mine in the world is near Tourney, Belgium; it is 3,542 feet in depth, but, unlike the lead mine mentioned above, it is not perpendicular. The deepest rock-salt bore in the world is near Berlin, Prussia; it is 4,185 feet deep. The deepest hole ever bored into the earth is the artesian well at Pottsdam, which is 5,500 feet in depth. The deepest coal mines in England are the Dunkirk colleries of Lancashire, which are 2,824 feet in depth. The deepest coal shaft in the United States is located at Pottsville, Pa. In 1885 it had reached a depth of 1,576 feet. From this great depth 400 cars, holding four tons each, are hoisted daily. The deepest silver mine in the United States is the Yellow Jacket, one of the great Comstock system at Virginia City, Nevada; the lower levels are 2,700 feet below the hoisting works.

FATE OF THE APOSTLES.—The following brief history of the fate of the Apostles may be new to those whose reading has not been evangelical:

St. Matthew is supposed to have suffered martyrdom or was slain with the sword at the city of Ethiopia.

St. Mark was dragged through the streets of Alexandria, in Egypt, till he expired.

St. Luke was hanged upon an olive tree in Greece.

St. John was put into a cauldron of boiling oil at Rome and escaped death. He afterward died a natural death at Ephesus in Asia.

St. James the Great was beheaded at Jerusalem.

St. James the Less was thrown from a pinnacle or wing of the temple and then beaten to death with a fuller's club.

St. Philip was hanged up against a pillar at Hieropolis, a city of Phrygia.

St. Bartholomew was flayed alive by the command of a barbarous king.

St. Andrew was bound to a cross, whence he preached unto the people until he expired.

St. Thomas was run through the body with a lance at Caromandel, in the East Indias.

St. Jude was shot to death with arrows.

St. Simon Zealot was crucified in Persia.

St. Matthias was first stoned and then beheaded.

St. Barnabas was stoned to death by Jews at Salania.

St. Paul was beheaded at Rome by the tyrant Nero.

The capital of the United States has been located at different times at the following places: At Philadelphia from September 5, 1774, until December, 1776; at Baltimore from December 20, 1776, to March, 1777; at Philadelphia from March 4, 1777, to September, 1777; at Lancaster, Pa., from September 27, 1777, to September 30, 1777; at York, Pa., from September 30, 1777, to July, 1778; at Philadelphia from July 2, 1778, to June 30, 1783; at Princeton, N.J., June 30, 1783, to November 20, 1783; Annapolis, Md., November 26, 1783, to November 30, 1784; Trenton, from November, 1784, to January, 1785; New York from January 11, 1785, to

1790; then the seat of government was removed to Philadelphia, where it remained until 1800, since which time it has been in Washington.

## THE SINGLE TAX.

This idea was first formulated by Mr. Henry George in 1879, and has grown steadily in favor. Single tax men assert as a fundamental principle that all men are equally entitled to the use of the earth; therefore, no one should be allowed to hold valuable land without paying to the community the value of the privilege. They hold that this is the only rightful source of public revenue, and they would therefore abolish all taxation—local, State and National—except a tax upon the rental value of land exclusive of its improvements, the revenue thus raised to be divided among local, State and general governments, as the revenue from certain direct taxes is now divided between local and State governments.

The single tax would not fall on all land, but only on valuable land, and on that in proportion to its value. It would thus be a tax, not on use or improvements, but on ownership of land, taking what would otherwise go to the landlord as owner.

In accordance with the principle that all men are equally entitled to the use of the earth, they would solve the transportation problem by public ownership and control of all highways, including the roadbeds of railroads, leaving their use equally free to all.

The single tax system would, they claim, dispense with a hoard of tax-gatherers, simplify government, and greatly reduce its cost; give us with all the world that absolute free trade which now exists between the States of the Union; abolish all taxes on private uses of money; take the weight of taxation from agricultural districts, where land has little or no value apart from improvements, and put it upon valuable land, such as city lots and mineral deposits. It would call upon men to contribute for public expenses in proportion to the natural opportunities they monopolize, and make it unprofitable for speculators to hold land unused, or only partly used, thus opening to labor unlimited fields of employment, solving the labor problem and abolishing involuntary poverty.

## VALUE OF FOREIGN COINS.
### Proclaimed by Law, January 1, 1891.

| Country. | Monetary Units | Standard. | Value in U.S. Money |
|---|---|---|---|
| Argentine Republic | Peso | Gold and Silver | $ .96 5-10 |
| Austria | Florin | Silver | .38 1-10 |
| Belgium | Franc | Gold and Silver | .19 3-10 |
| Bolivia | Boliviano | Silver | .77 1-10 |
| Brazil | Milreis | Gold | .54 6-10 |
| Canada | Dollar | Gold | 1.00 |
| Chili | Peso | Gold and Silver | .91 2-10 |
| China | Tael | Silver | 1.27 |
| Cuba | Peso | Gold and Silver | .92 6-10 |
| Denmark | Crown | Gold | .26 8-10 |
| Ecuador | Peso | Silver | .77 1-10 |
| Egypt | Piaster | Gold | .04 9-10 |
| France | Franc | Gold and Silver | .19 3-10 |
| Great Britain | Pound Sterling | Gold | 4.86 6-100 |
| Greece | Drachma | Gold and Silver | .19 3-10 |
| erman Empire | Mark | Gold | .23 8-10 |
| Hayti | Gourde | Gold and | .96 5-10 |

|  |  | Silver |  |
| --- | --- | --- | --- |
| India | Rupee | Silver | .36 6-10 |
| Italy | Lira | Gold and Silver | .19 3-10 |
| Japan | Yen | Silver | .85 8-10 |
| Liberia | Dollar | Gold | 1.00 |
| Mexico | Dollar | Silver | .83 7-10 |
| Netherlands | Florin | Gold and Silver | .40 2-10 |
| Norway | Crown | Gold | .26 8-10 |
| Peru | Sol | Silver | .77 1-10 |
| Portugal | Milreis | Gold | 1.08 |
| Russia | Rouble | Silver | .61 7-10 |
| Sandwich Islands | Dollar | Gold | 1.00 |
| Spain | Peseta | Gold and Silver | .19 3-10 |
| Sweden | Crown | Gold | .26 8-10 |
| Switzerland | Franc | Gold and Silver | .19 3-10 |
| Tripoli | Mahbub | Silver | .69 5-10 |
| Turkey | Piaster | Gold | .04 4-10 |
| U.S. of Columbia | Peso | Silver | .79 5-10 |
| Venezuela | Bolivar | Gold and Silver | .15 4-10 |

The largest producing farm in the world lies in the southwest corner of Louisiana, owned by a northern syndicate. It runs one hundred miles north and south. The immense tract is divided into convenient pastures, with stations of ranches every six miles. The fencing alone cost nearly $50,000.

The "Seven Wonders of the World" are seven most remarkable objects of the ancient world. They are: The Pyramids of Egypt, Pharos of Alexandria,

Walls and Hanging Gardens of Babylon, Temple of Diana at Ephesus, the Statue of the Olympian Jupiter, Mausoleum of Artemisia, and Colossus of Rhodes.

The seven sages flourished in Greece in the 6th century B.C. They were renowned for their maxims of life and as the authors of the mottoes inscribed in the Delphian Temple. Their names are: Solon, Chilo, Pittacus, Bias, Periander, Clebolus and Thales.

The estimated number of Christians in the world is over 408,000,000; of Buddhists, 420,000,000; of the followers of Brahma, 180,000,000; of Mohammedans, 150,000,000; of Jews, 8,000,000; of atheists, deists, and infidels, 85,000,000; of pagans, 50,000,000, and of the 1,100 other minor creeds, 123,000,000.

In 1775 there were only 27 newspapers published in the United States. Ten years later, in 1785, there were seven published in the English language in Philadelphia alone, of which one was a daily. The oldest newspaper published in Philadelphia at the time of the Federal convention was the *Pennsylvania Gazette*, established by Samuel Keimer, in 1728. The second newspaper in point of age was the *Pennsylvania Journal*, established in 1742 by William Bradford, whose uncle, Andrew Bradford, established the first newspaper in Pennsylvania, the *American Weekly Mercury*, in 1719. The next in age, but the first in importance, was the *Pennsylvania Packet*, established by John Dunlop in 1771. In 1784 it became a daily, being the first daily newspaper printed on this continent.

# GEMS OF THOUGHT.

## POOR RICHARD'S ALMANAC
## BY
## Benjamin Franklin.

## POOR RICHARD'S ALMANAC.

COURTEOUS READER:

I have heard that nothing gives an author so great pleasure as to find his works respectfully quoted by other learned authors. This pleasure I have seldom enjoyed. For though I have been, if I may say it without vanity, an *eminent* author of *Almanacs* annually now for a full quarter of a century, my brother authors in the same way, for what reason I know not, have ever been very sparing in their applauses; and no other author has taken the least notice of me; so that did not my writings produce me some solid pudding, the great deficiency of praise would have quite discouraged me.

I concluded at length that the people were the best judges of my merit, for they buy my works; and besides, in my rambles where I am not personally known, I have frequently heard one or other of my adages repeated, with *as Poor Richard says* at the end of it. This gives me some satisfaction, as it showed, not only that my instructions were regarded, but discovered likewise some respect for my authority; and I own that to encourage the practice of remembering and repeating those sentences, I have sometimes quoted myself with great activity.

Judge, then, how much I must have been gratified by an incident I am going to relate to you. I stopped my horse lately where a great number of people were collected at a vendue of merchant's goods. The hour of sale not being come, they were conversing on the badness of the times; and one of the company called to a plain, clean old man with white locks, "Pray, Father Abraham, what think you of the times? Won't these heavy taxes quite ruin the country? How shall we ever be able to pay them? What would you advise us to do?" Father Abraham stood up and replied: "If you would have my advice, I will give it you in short; for *A word to the wise is enough*, and *Many words won't fill a bushel*, as Poor Richard says." They all joined, desiring him to speak his mind, and gathering round him, he proceeded as follows:

Friends, says he, and neighbors, the taxes are indeed very heavy, and if those laid on by the government were the only ones we had to pay, we might the more easily discharge them; but we have many others, and much more grievous to some of us. We are taxed twice as much by our IDLENESS, three times as much by our PRIDE and four times as much by our FOLLY; and from these taxes the commissioners cannot ease or deliver us, by allowing an abatement. However, let us hearken to good advice, and something may be done for us; *God helps them that help themselves*, as Poor Richard says in his *Almanac* of 1733.

It would be thought a hard government that should tax its people one-tenth part of their TIME, to be employed in its service, but idleness taxes many of us much more, if we reckon all that is spent in absolute sloth, or doing of nothing, with that which is spent in idle employments or amusements that amount to nothing. Sloth, by bringing on disease, absolutely shortens life. *Sloth, like rust, consumes faster than labor wears; while the used key is always bright*, as Poor Richard says. *But dost thou love life? Then do not squander time, for that's the stuff life is made of*, as Poor Richard says.

How much more that is necessary do we spend in sleep? Forgetting that *the sleeping fox catches no poultry,* and that *there will be sleeping enough in the grave,* as Poor Richard says. If times be of all things the most precious, *wasting of time must be,* as Poor Richard says, *the greatest prodigality;* since, as he elsewhere tells us, *lost time is never found again*; and what we call *time enough! always proves little enough.* Let us then up and be doing, and doing to the purpose; so, by diligence, shall we do more with less perplexity. *Sloth makes all things difficult, but industry all things easy,* as Poor Richard says; and *He that riseth late must trot all day, and shall scarce overtake his business at night; while laziness travels so slowly that Poverty soon overtakes him,* as we read in Poor Richard; who adds, *Drive thy business! Let not that drive thee!* and

> Early to bed and early to rise
> Makes a man healthy, wealthy and wise.

So what signifies *wishing* and *hoping* for better times? We may make these times better if we bestir ourselves. *Industry need not wish,* as Poor Richard says, and *He that lives on hope will die fasting. There are no gains without pains; then help, hands! for I have no lands*; or if I have they are smartly taxed. And, as Poor Richard likewise observes, *He that hath a trade hath an estate, and he that hath a calling hath an honor*; but then the trade must be worked at, and the calling well followed, or neither the estate nor the office will enable us to pay our taxes. If we are industrious we shall never starve; for, as Poor Richard says, *At the working-man's house hunger looks in, but dares not enter.* Nor will the bailiff or the constable enter, for *Industry pays debts, while despair increaseth them.*

What though you have found no treasure, nor has any rich relation left you a legacy, *Diligence is the mother of good luck,* as Poor Richard says, *and God gives all things to industry*

> Then plough deep while the sluggards sleep,
> And you shall have corn to sell and to keep,

says Poor Dick. Work while it is called to-day, for you know not how much you may be hindered to-morrow; which makes Poor Richard say, *One to-*

*day is worth two to-morrows*; and farther, *Have you somewhat to do tomorrow? Do it to-day!*

If you were a servant, would you not be ashamed that a good master should catch you idle? Are you then your own master? *Be ashamed to catch yourself idle*, as Poor Richard says. When there is so much to be done for yourself, your family, your country, and your gracious king, be up by peep of day! *Let not the sun look down and say, "Inglorious here he lies!"* Handle your tools without mittens! remember that *The cat in gloves catches no mice!* as poor Richard says.

'Tis true there is much to be done, and perhaps you are weak-handed; but stick to it steadily, and you will see great effects; for *Constant dropping wears away stones*; and *By diligence and patience the mouse ate in two the cable*; and *Little strokes fell great oaks*; as Poor Richard says in his *Almanac*, the year I cannot just now remember.

Methinks I hear some of you say, "Must a man afford himself no leisure?" I will tell, thee, my friend, what Poor Richard says, *Employ thy time well, if thou meanest to gain leisure*; and *Since thou are not sure of a minute, throw not away an hour!* Leisure is time for doing something useful; this leisure the diligent man will obtain, but the lazy man never; so that, as Poor Richard says, *A life of leisure and a life of laziness are two things.* Do you imagine that sloth will afford you more comfort than labor? No! for as Poor Richard says, *Trouble springs from idleness, and grievous toil from needless ease. Many, without labor, would live by their wits only, but they'll break for want of stock* (i.e. capital); whereas industry gives comfort, and plenty, and respect. *Fly pleasures, and they'll follow you. The diligent spinner has a large shift*; and

>Now I have a sheep and a cow,
>Everybody bids me good morrow.

All which is well said by Poor Richard. But with our industry we must likewise be steady, settled, and careful, and oversee our own affairs *with our own eyes*, and not trust too much to others; for, as Poor Richard says,

> I never saw an oft removed tree,
> Nor yet an oft removed family,
> That throve so well as those that settled be.

And again, *Three removes are as bad as a fire*; and again, *Keep thy shop, and thy shop will keep thee*; and again, *If you would have your business done, go; if not, send.* And again,

> He that by the plough would thrive,
> Himself must either hold or drive.

And again, *The eye of the master will do more work than both his hands*; and again, *Want of care does us more damage than want of knowledge*; and again, *Not to oversee workmen is to leave them your purse open.*

Trusting too much to others' care is the ruin of many; for, as the Almanac says, *In the affairs of this world men are saved, not by faith, but by the want of it*; but a man's own care is profitable; for saith Poor Dick, *Learning is to the studious and Riches to the careful*; as well as, *Power to the bold, and Heaven to the virtuous.* And further, *If you would have a faithful servant, and one that you like, serve yourself.*

And again, he adviseth to circumspection and care, even in the smallest matters; because, sometimes, *A little neglect may breed great mischief*; adding, *for want of a nail the shoe was lost; for want of a shoe the horse was lost; and for want of a horse the rider was lost*; being overtaken and slain by the enemy; all for want of a little care about a horseshoe nail!

So much for industry, my friends, and attention to one's own business; but to these we must add frugality, if we would make our industry more certainly successful. *A man may*, if he knows not how to save as he gets, *keep his nose all his life to the grindstone, and die not worth a groat at last. A fat kitchen makes a lean will*, as Poor Richard says; and

> Many estates are spent in the getting,
> Since women for tea[3] forsook spinning and knitting,
> And men for punch forsook hewing and splitting.

If you would be wealthy, says he in another Almanac, *Think of saving as well as of getting. The Indies have not made Spain rich; because her outgoes are greater than her incomes.*

Away, then, with your expensive follies, and you will not have so much cause to complain of hard times, heavy taxes, and chargeable families; for, as Poor Dick says,—

> Women and wine, game and deceit,
> Make the wealth small and the wants great.

And farther, *What maintains one vice would bring up two children.* You may think, perhaps, that a *little* tea, or a *little* punch now and then; a diet a *little* more mostly; clothes a *little* more finer; and a *little* more entertainment now and then, can be no great matter; but remember what Poor Richard says, *Many a little makes a mickle*; and further, *Beware of little expenses; A small leak will sink a great ship*; and again,—

> Who dainties love, shall beggars prove;

and moreover, *Fools make feasts and wise men eat them.*

Here are you all got together at this vendue of fineries knick-knacks. You call them *goods*; but if you do not take care, they will prove evils to some of you. You expect they will be sold cheap, and perhaps they may for less than they cost; but, if you have no occasion for them, they must be *dear* to you. Remember what Poor Richard says: *Buy what thou hast no need of and ere long thou shalt sell thy necessaries.* And again, *At a great pennyworth, pause a while.* He means, that perhaps the cheapness is apparent only, and not real; or the bargain by straitening thee in thy business, may do thee more harm than good. For in another place he says, *Many have been ruined by buying good pennyworths.*

Again, Poor Richard says, *'Tis foolish to lay out money in a purchase of repentance*; and yet this folly is practiced every day at vendues for want of minding the *Almanac*.

*Wise men,* as Poor Richard says, *learn by others' harms; Fools scarcely by their own*; but *Felix quem faciunt aliena pericula cautum.*[4] Many a one for the sake of finery on the back, has gone with a hungry belly, and half-starved their families. *Silks and satins, scarlets and velvets,* as Poor Richard says, *put out the kitchen fire*. These are not the necessaries of life; they can scarcely be called the conveniences; and yet, only because they look pretty, how many *want* to have them! The artificial wants of mankind thus become more numerous than the natural; and, as Poor Dick says, *For one* poor *person there are a hundred* indigent.

By these and other extravagances, the genteel are reduced to poverty, and forced to borrow of those whom they formerly despised, but who, through industry and frugality, have maintained their standing; in which case it appears plainly, that *A ploughman on his legs is higher than a gentleman on his knees*, as Poor Richard says. Perhaps they have had a small estate left them, which they know not the getting of; they think, *'Tis day, and will never be night,* that a *little to be spent out of so much is not worth minding*; (*A child and a fool,* as Poor Richard says, *imagine* twenty shilling and twenty years can never be spent), but *Always taking out of the meal-tub and never putting in, soon comes to the bottom*. Then, as Poor Dick says, *When the well's dry, they know the worth of water*. But this they might have known before, if they had taken his advice. *If you would know the value of money, go and try to borrow some;* for *He that goes a borrowing, goes a sorrowing,* and indeed, so does he that lends to such people, *when he goes to get it again*.

Poor Dick further advises and says—

> Fond pride of dress is, sure a very curse;
> Ere fancy you consult, consult your purse.

And again, *Pride is as loud a beggar as Want, and a great deal more saucy.* When you have bought one fine thing, you must buy ten more, that your appearance may be all of a piece; but Poor Dick says, *'Tis easier to suppress the first desire than to satisfy all that follow it.* And 'tis as truly folly for the poor to ape the rich, as for the frog to swell in order to equal the ox.

> Great estates may venture more,
> But little boats should keep near shore.

'Tis, however, a folly soon punished; for, *Pride that dines on vanity sups on contempt*, as Poor Richard says. And in another place, *Pride breakfasted with Plenty, dined with Poverty and supped with Infancy.*

And after all, what use is this pride of appearance, for which so much is risked, so much is suffered? It cannot promote health or ease pain; it makes no increase of merit in the person; it creates envy; it hastens misfortune.

> What is a butterfly? At best
> He's but a caterpillar drest,
> The gaudy fop's his picture just,

as poor Richard says.

But what madness must it be to *run into debt* for these superfluities! We are offered, by the terms of this vendue, six months' credit; and that, perhaps, has induced some of us to attend it, because we cannot spare the ready money, and hope now to be fine without it. But, ah! think what you do when you run in debt: *You give to another power over your liberty.* If you cannot pay at the time, you will be ashamed to see your creditor; you will be in fear when you speak to him; you will make poor, pitiful, sneaking excuses, and by degrees come to lose our veracity, and sink into base, downright lying; for, as Poor Richard says, *The second vice is lying, the first is running into debt*; and again, to the same purpose, *lying rides upon debt's back*; whereas a free-born Englishman ought not to be ashamed or afraid to see or speak to any man living. But poverty often deprives a man of all spirit and virtue. *'Tis hard for an empty bag to stand upright!* as Poor

Richard truly says. What would you think of that prince, or that government who should issue an edict forbidding you to dress like a gentleman or gentlewoman, on pain of imprisonment or servitude? Would you not say that you are free, have a right to dress as you please, and that such an edict would be a breach of your privileges, and such a government tyranical? And yet you are about to put yourself under such tyranny, when you run in debt for such dress! Your creditor has authority, at his pleasure, to deprive you of your liberty, by confining you in jail for life, or to sell you for a servant, if you should not be able to pay him.[5] When you have got your bargain you may, perhaps, think little of payment; but *Creditors* (Poor Richard tells us) *have better memories than debtors*; and in another place says, *Creditors are a superstitious set, great observers of set days and times.* The day comes round before you are aware, and the demand is made before you are prepared to satisfy it; or, if you will bear your debt in mind, the term which at first seemed so long will, as it lessens, appear extremely short. Time will seem to have added wings to his heels as well as his shoulders. *Those have a short Lent*, saith Poor Richard, *who owe money to be paid at Easter.* Then since, as he says, *The borrower is a slave to the lender, and the debtor to the creditor*, disdain the chain, preserve your freedom, and maintain your independency. Be *industrious* and *free*; be *frugal* and *free*. At present, perhaps, you may think yourself in thriving circumstances, and that you can bear a little extravagance without injury; but—

> For age and want, save while you may,
> No morning sun lasts a whole day.

As Poor Richard says, gain may be temporary and uncertain; but ever, while you live, expense is constant and certain; and *'Tis easier to build two chimneys than to keep one in fuel*, as Poor Richard says; so, *Rather go to bed supperless than rise in debt.*

> Get what you can and what you get hold:
> 'Tis the stone that will turn all your lead in gold,[6]

as Poor Richard says; and, while you have got the Philosopher's stone, sure, you will no longer complain of bad times or the difficulty of paying taxes.

This doctrine, my friends, is reason and wisdom; but, after all, do not depend too much upon your own industry and frugality and prudence, though excellent things; for they may all be blasted without the blessing of Heaven; and therefore, ask that blessing humbly, and be not uncharitable to those that at present seem to want it, but comfort and help them. Remember Job suffered, and was afterwards prosperous.

And now, to conclude, *Experience keeps a dear school, but fools will learn in no other, and scarce in that*; for it is true, *We may give advice, but we cannot give conduct*, as Poor Richard says. However, remember this, *They that won't be counselled, can't be helped*, as Poor Richard says; and further, that, *If you will not hear reason, she'll surely rap your knuckles.*

Thus the old gentleman ended his harangue. The people heard it, and approved the doctrine; and immediately practiced the contrary, just as if it had been a common sermon. For the vendue opened, and they began to buy extravagantly, notwithstanding all his cautions, and their own fear of taxes. I found the good man had thoroughly studied my *Almanacs*, and digested all I had dropped on those topics during the course of five-and-twenty-years. The frequent mention he made of me must have tired any one else; but my vanity was wonderfully delighted with it, though I was conscious that not a tenth part of the wisdom was my own which he ascribed to me, but rather the gleanings that I had made of the sense of all ages and nations. However, I resolved to be the better for the echo of it; and, though I had at first determined to buy stuff for a new coat, I went away resolved to wear my old one a little longer. Reader, if thou wilt do the same, *thy* profit will be as great as mine. I am, as ever, thine to serve thee.

July 7, 1757.

RICHARD SAUNDERS.

### THE WATER-MILL.

Oh! listen to the water-mill, through all the live-long day,
As the clicking of the wheels wears hour by hour away;
How languidly the autumn wind doth stir the withered leaves,
As on the field the reapers sing, while binding up the sheaves!
A solemn proverb strikes my mind, and as a spell is cast,
"The mill will never grind again with water that is past."

The summer winds revive no more leaves strewn o'er earth and main,
The sickle never more will reap the yellow garnered grain;
The rippling stream flows on, aye tranquil, deep, and still,
But never glideth back again to busy water-mill.
The solemn proverb speaks to all, with meaning deep and vast,
"The mill will never grind again with water that is past."

Oh! clasp the proverb to thy soul, dear loving heart and true,
For golden years are fleeting by, and youth is passing, too;
Ah! learn to make the most of life, nor lose one happy day,
For time will ne'er return sweet joys neglected, thrown away;
Nor leave one tender word unsaid, thy kindness sow broadcast

"The mill will never grind again with water that is past."

Oh! the wasted hours of life, that have swiftly drifted by,
Alas! the good we might have done, all gone without a sigh;
Love that we might once have saved by a single kindly word,
Thoughts conceived but ne'er expressed, perishing unpenned, unheard.
Oh! take the lesson to thy soul, forever clasp it fast,
"The mill will never grind again with water that is past."

Work on while yet the sun doth shine, thou man of strength and will,
The streamlet ne'er doth useless glide by clicking watermill;
Nor wait until to-morrow's light beams brightly on thy way.
For all that thou canst call thine own, lies in the phrase, "to-day;"
Possessions, power, and blooming health, must all be lost at last —

"The mill will never grind again with water that is past."

Oh! love thy God and fellow man, thyself consider last,
For come it will when they must scan dark errors of the past;
Soon will this fight of life be o'er, and earth recede from view,
And heaven in all its glory shine where all is pure and true.
Ah! then thou'lt see more clearly still the proverb deep and vast,
"The mill will never grind again with water that is past."

               D. C. McCallum.

---

Is life so dear, or peace so sweet, as to be purchased at the price of chains and slavery? Forbid it, Almighty God! I know not what course others may take, but for me, give me liberty or give me death.

PATRICK HENRY.

The law is a sort of hocus-pocus science, that smiles in yer face while it picks yer pocket; and the glorious uncertainty of it is of mair use to the professors than the justice of it.

MACKLIN.

## OUR MISSION.

In calm and stormy weather
    Our mission is to grow;
To keep the angle paramount
    And bind the brute below.

We grow not all in sunshine,
    But richly in the rain;
And what we deem our losses
    May prove our final gain.

The snows and frosts of winter
    A richer fruitage bring;
From battling with the anvil
    The smith's grand muscles spring.

'Tis by the law of contrast
    That fine effects are seen;
As thus we blend in colors
    The orange with the green.

By action and reaction
    We reach our perfect growth;
Nor by excess of neither,

But equipoise of both.
The same code binds the human.

   That governs mother earth;
God cradled her in tempest
   And earthquakes from her birth.

Our life is but a struggle
   For perfect equipoise;
Our pains are often jewels,
   Our pleasures gilded toys.

Between the good and evil
   The monarch will must stand,
To shape the final issue
   By God's divine command.

Our mission is to battle
   With ill in every form—
To borrow strength and volume
   From contact with the storm.

In the beautiful hereafter
   These blinding mortal tears
Shall crystalize in jewels
   To sparkle in the spheres.

With weak and moldish vision
   We work our way below;
But sure our souls are building
   Much wiser than we know.

And when the work is finished
   The scaffolding then falls;
And lo! a radiant temple,

> With pearl and sapphire walls.
>
> A temple far transcending
>    The grandest piles below,
> Whose dome shall blaze with splendor,
>    In God's eternal glow.

Wealth is necessary; let us not disclaim against it; every nation needs it to attain the highest achievements in civilization. But it is a blessing only as a servant, and is destructive as a master.

JOHN P. ALTGELD.

If I were a young man I should ally myself with some high and at present unpopular cause, and devote my every effort to accomplish its success.

JOHN G. WHITTIER.

> Ill fares the land, to hastening ills a prey,
>    Where wealth accumulates and men decay.
>
> Princes and lords may flourish and may fade;
> A breath can make them, as breath has made;
> But an honest peasantry, a country's pride,
> When once destroyed, can never be supplied.

War preys on two things—life and property: but he preys with a partial appetite. Feasting on life, he licks his jaws and says, "More, by your leave!" Devouring property, he says, between grin and glut, "This is so good that it ought to be paid for!" Into the vacuum of wasted life rush the moaning winds of grief and desolation; in to the vacuum of wasted property rushes the goblin of debt. The wasted life is transformed at length into a reminiscent glory; the wasted property becomes a hideous nightmare. The heroes fallen rise from their bloody cerements into everlasting fame; the property destroyed rises from the red and flame-swept field as a spectral vampire, sucking the still warm blood of the heroic dead and of their posthumous babes to the tenth generation! The name of the vampire is Bond.

JOHN CLARK RIDPATH.

## TO A WATERFOWL.

Whither, mid'st falling dew,
While glow the heavens with the last steps of day,
Far through their rosy depths, dost thou pursue
    Thy solitary way?

Vainly the fowler's eye
Might mark thy distant flight to do thee wrong,
As, darkly seen against the crimson sky,
    Thy figure floats along.

Seek'st thou the plashy brink
Of weedy lake, or marge of river wide,
Or where the rocking billows rise and sink
    On the chafed ocean side?

There is a Power whose care
Teaches thy way along that pathless coast—
The desert and illimitable air—
    Lone wandering, but not lost.

All day thy wings have fanned,
At that far height, the cold, thin atmosphere,
Yet stoop not, weary, to the welcome land,
Though the dark night is near.

And soon that toil shall end;
Soon shalt thou find a summer home, and rest,
And scream among thy fellows; reeds shall bend
Soon, o'er thy sheltered nest.

Thou'rt gone, the abyss of heaven
Hath swallowed up thy form; yet on my heart
Deeply hath sunk the lesson thou hast given
And shall not soon depart.

He who, from zone to zone,
Guides through the boundless sky thy certain flight,
In the long way that I must tread alone
Will lead my steps aright.

WILLIAM CULLEN BRYANT.

## ROBERT BURNS

(Considered by many the world's greatest Song writer and natural Poet.)

While Burns was yet a plow boy he was challenged by two highly educated gentlemen, who were seated awaiting their dinner to be served at an Inn in the town of Ayr.

The terms of the challenge was for each to write a verse on the event of their first acquaintance, the one writing the best and most appropriate short rhyme was to have his dinner paid for by the other two.

Burns wrote as follows:

> I Jonnie Peep,
> Saw two sheep.
> Two sheep saw me.
> Half a crown apiece
> Will pay for their fleece.
> And I Jonnie Peep go free.

On another occasion while drinking at a Bar a hanger on who was notorious for his much drinking and was dubbed the Marquis, asked Burns to write an appropriate epitaph for his grave stone.

Burns, quick as flash and without any apparent effort, wrote:

> Here lies a faulse Marquis:
> Whose title is shamed
> If ever he rises
> It will be to be damned.

## TO A MOUSE.

> Wee, sleekit, cowrin' tim'rous beastie.
> Oh, what a panic's in thy breastie!
> Thou needna start awa' sae hasty.
>     Wi' bickering brattle!
> I wad be laith to rin and chase thee,
>     Wi murd'ing prattle!
>
> I'm truly sorry man's dominion
> Has broken nature's social union,
> And justifies that ill opinion

Which makes thee startle
At me, thy poor earth-born companion
      And fellow-mortal!

I doubt na, whiles, but thou may thieve;
What then? poor beastie, thou maun live!
A daimen icker in a thrave
      'S a sma' o' request
I'll get a blessin' wi' the lave,
      And never miss 't!

Thy wee bit housie, too, in ruin!
Its silly wa's the win's are strewin'!
And naething now to big a new ane
      O' foggage green!
And bleak December's winds ensuin'
      Baith snell and keen!

Thou saw the fields laid bare and waste
And weary winter comin' fast.
And cozie here, beneath the blast,
      Thou thought to dwell;
Till, crash! the cruel coulter past
      Out through thy cell.

That wee bit heap o'leaves and stibble
Has cost thee mony a weary nibble!
Now thou's turn'd out for a' thy trouble,
      But house or hauld,
To thole the winter's sleety dribble
      And cranreuch cauld.

www.ingramcontent.com/pod-product-compliance
Lightning Source LLC
Chambersburg PA
CBHW081111080526
44587CB00021B/3540